The SUNDAY POST

FAMILY

QUIZ BOOK

No.1

Printed and published by D.C. THOMSON & CO., LTD.,
185 Fleet Street, London EC4A 2HS.
© D.C. THOMSON & CO., LTD., 2007

ISBN 9 781845 353452

GENERAL KNOWLEDGE

How much do YOU know?

● 1-5 Know a little! ● 6-11 Know a lot! ● 12-16 Know it all!

1. What sort of creature is a Sealyham?
2. Name three actors who've portrayed Sherlock Holmes in the cinema or on TV.
3. Which Scottish city has given its name to a Hong Kong harbour?
4. What is meant by the Scottish word, glaur?
5. Which US state is sometimes known as the 'Evergreen' state?
6. Which tough-skinned larva sounds as if it could also be found in a clothing shop?
7. Rearrange FILE CHEF LIFE PERM to identify a popular Hollywood celebrity.
8. Name the famous son of American musical star Mary Martin.
9. Which member of the Royal Family is the Earl of Chester?
10. In the UK we call it draughts, but by what name is it known in the USA?
11. Solve these 'par' words: a) mental condition of extreme distrust, b) culinary herb, c) prisoner's temporary release.
12. Where was Lusitania?
13. In TV's *The Good Life* who lived next door to Tom and Barbara Good?
14. Why should you never stifle a sneeze?
15. If you suffer from brontophobia what kind of weather do you fear?
16. Name Popeye's son.

ANSWERS

1 A dog, 2 Basil Rathbone, Peter Cushing, Jeremy Brett, Edward Woodward, Stewart Granger etc, 3 Aberdeen, 4 Soft, sticky mud, 5 Washington, 6 A leatherjacket — it's the larva of the crane fly, 7 Michelle Pfeiffer, 8 Larry Hagman, 9 Prince Charles, 10 Checkers, 11 a) Paranoia, b) parsley, c) parole, 12 It was a Roman province, now in Portugal and Spain, 13 Margo and Jerry Leadbetter, 14 Because it prevents the clearance of germs and pressure could damage your ears, 15 Thunder, 16 Swee'Pea.

SPORT
Fit and healthy!

1. What nationality is golfer Ernie Els?
2. How old was Olga Korbut when she competed in the 1972 Olympic Games?
3. With which sport was Gillian Gilks associated?
4. What was boxer Nigel Benn's nickname?
5. In which year did sprinter Alan Wells win a gold medal in the Olympic 100 metres?
6. Which baseball player was known as the Yankee Clipper?
7. Who was the first Welshman to win the World Snooker title?
8. Which West Indian batsman announced his retirement after the 2007 World Cup?
9. In which year did the first football World Cup take place?
10. In which country were the 1998 Winter Olympics held?
11. Where would you find American Football team the Dolphins?
12. Who scored the goal that clinched the Premier League title for Celtic in April, 2007?
13. In which year did Tony Jacklin win the US Open Golf Championship?
14. What is the length of a table-tennis table? Eight feet, nine feet or ten feet?
15. When did Sir Alex Ferguson become manager of Manchester United?
16. In which city was tennis player Monica Seles stabbed?

ANSWERS

1 South African, 2 17, 3 Badminton, 4 The Dark Destroyer, 5 1980, 6 Joe DiMaggio, 7 Ray Reardon, 8 Brian Lara, 9 1930, 10 Japan, 11 Miami, 12 Shunsuke Nakamura, 13 1970, 14 Nine feet, 15 1986, 16 Hamburg.

GENERAL KNOWLEDGE

Facts are fun!

● 1-5 Could improve! ● 6-11 Getting better! ● 12-16 The best!

1. Which British coin has the motto 'standing on the shoulders of giants' on its edge?
2. If you ordered l'ananas in a French restaurant what would you be served?
3. What would you do with a pasanda — eat it, keep it in the zoo or play a tune on it?
4. When might you hear a siren coming from your phone?
5. Which classic British car, introduced in the 1950s, was known as a 'woody'?
6. Name Elvis Presley's first movie.
7. In the disease CJD, C is for Creutzfeldt, but what does J stand for?
8. What is Old Faithful in Yellowstone National Park, Wyoming?
9. Which Irish town is famous for its crystal glass?
10. In which US TV show do characters shop at the Kwik-E-Mart?
11. Name five things that are mined.
12. How is nitrous oxide more commonly known?
13. Match up the dog breeds Shih Tzu, Lhasa Apso, Weimaraner and Beagle with their countries of origin, which are China, England, Tibet and Germany.
14. Why do potatoes have eyes?
15. Do your pupils grow larger or smaller in dim light?
16. If you spend more than you earn you're said to be 'in the red'. Why?

ANSWERS

1 The £2 coin, 2 Pineapple, 3 Eat it, it's a curry, 4 When it has been left off the hook, 5 Morris Minor Traveller, because its bodywork was framed in wood, 6 I Love Me Tender in 1956, 7 Jakob, 8 A geyser, 9 Waterford, 10 The Simpsons, 11 Diamonds, coal, tin, gold, lead etc, 12 Laughing gas, 13 Shih Tzu — China, Lhasa Apso — Tibet, Weimaraner — Germany, Beagle — England, 14 They're buds which produce the shoots of new stems, 15 Larger, 16 Accountants and bankers traditionally wrote losses in red ink.

GENERAL KNOWLEDGE
Take the test.

1. John Logie Baird, inventor of television, was born in 1888 — but where?
2. What does the award KBE stand for?
3. On the phone, what happens if you dial 141 before the number you're calling?
4. Which vitamin is known as the retinol vitamin — A, C or D?
5. In Germany, how would a kapellmeister earn his living?
6. Rearrange LAIRD OF SKYE to discover a holiday resort in southern USA.
7. Which Scottish city hosted the 1986 Commonwealth Games?
8. On the top line of a computer keyboard, how many letters lie between Q and P?
9. What is a boomer in Australia?
10. Which is higher — Blackpool Tower or BT Tower in London?
11. Make a connection between Little Eva and Kylie Minogue.
12. What should you use a hassock for?
13. Name the last state to join the USA.
14. How many Books of The Bible begin with D?
15. Which international organisation is identified by a candle in barbed wire?
16. How many brothers and sisters does Michael Jackson have?

ANSWERS

1 Helensburgh, 2 Knight Commander of the Order of the British Empire, 3 Your number is withheld, 4 Vitamin A, 5 By leading an orchestra or choir, 6 Florida Keys, 7 Edinburgh, 8 Eight (W, E, R, T, Y, U, I, O), 9 A male kangaroo, 10 BT Tower at 620 ft. Blackpool Tower is 519 ft, 11 Both had hits with the song The Locomotion, 12 Kneeling on — it's a low padded stool, used in churches etc, 13 Hawaii became the 50th state on August 21, 1959, 14 Two, Daniel and Deuteronomy etc, 15 Amnesty International, 16 He's the seventh of nine children — brothers Jackie, Tito, Jermaine, Marlon, Randy, and sisters Rebbie, Janet and La-Toya.

THE SUNDAY POST FAMILY QUIZ BOOK

ENTERTAINMENT
Test your celebrity rating.

1. In the art world, what does 'fresco' mean?
2. Which comedian used the phrase 'Rock On Tommy'?
3. 'Hasta La Vista, Baby' is a quote from which Arnold Schwarzenegger film?
4. In the card game Canasta, what is the value of the Joker – 25, 35 or 50 points?
5. What's the connection between Eddie Murphy and Phillip Scofield?
6. In the world of celebrities, Jilly, Henry and Tommy shared the same surname. What was it?
7. What would you do with a zither?
8. How many basic ballet positions are there – 5, 7 or 12?
9. What is the correct term for the Actors' Union?
10. Is a mazurka a Polish dance, drink or costume?
11. How many spots are there on a dice?
12. Which cartoon strip features Linus, Lucy, Shroeder and Woodstock?
13. Which post-war comedian used the catch-phrase 'Hello, Playmates!'?
14. In the *Dandy*, what is Desperate Dan's aunt called?
15. What does BAFTA stand for?
16. Can you name the first pirate radio station (established in 1964)?

ANSWERS

1 Painted directly onto a wall, 2 Bobby Ball (of his partner Tommy Cannon), 3 Terminator 2, 4 Fifty points, 5 Doctor Doolittle – Murphy starred in a Hollywood version, Scofield in a stage version, 6 Cooper, 7 Play it – it's a musical instrument, 8 Five, 9 Equity, 10 Dance, 11 Twenty-one, 12 Peanuts, 13 Arthur Askey, 14 Aunt Aggie, 15 British Academy of Film and Television Arts 16 Radio Caroline.

GENERAL KNOWLEDGE
Quite quizzical!

● 1-5 Quite quiet! ● 6-11 Quite qualified! ● 12-16 Quite quick!

1. Madame Tussaud of wax museum fame was born in which country?
2. What type of wood gets its name from the Spanish word for raft?
3. In the saying, there are none so deaf as whom?
4. Cavies are more commonly known as what?
5. The RS2000 is a special version of which popular car?
6. Name a plant that begins with something you have when you're running a temperature?
7. How did the American Sally Ride make headlines in 1983?
8. Rearrange SAM LEFT HOT ROD to find the name of a Scots engineer.
9. Which girl's name can follow North and South in a list of US states?
10. Why does someone who accepts responsibility 'carry the can'?
11. Name three ingredients added to mayonnaise to make a Waldorf salad.
12. How was Yugoslav leader Josip Broz better known?
13. The Stevie Wonder song *Happy Birthday To You* served as a tribute to whom?
14. What's unusual about sleeping snakes?
15. Finish this Longfellow line, 'I shot an arrow into the air____'
16 What nationality was the Scandinavian astronomer Anders Celsius?

ANSWERS

1 Strasbourg, France, in 1761, 2 Balsa wood, 3 Those who will not hear, 4 Guinea pigs, 5 The Ford Escort, 6 Feverfew, 7 She was America's first woman in space, 8 Thomas Telford, 9 Carolina, 10 'Forces' slang for someone who collected the rations in cans. He would be in trouble if he spilled anything, 11 Apples, celery and walnuts, 12 President Tito, 13 Martin Luther King, 14 They sleep with their eyes open, 15 It fell to earth, I know not where, 16 Swedish.

GENERAL KNOWLEDGE
How much do YOU know?

1. Why don't you enjoy your food so much when you have a cold?
2. In the Rocky series of films, what is Rocky's surname?
3. According to the proverb, what is the thief of time?
4. Rearrange FALTER to find an island off the Scottish coast.
5. Which European country's flag is blue and white stripes with a white cross on blue in the top left corner?
6. A zloty consisted of 100 groszes in which European country?
7. What is a boot camp in America?
8. Starting in the centre, name the five colours found on an archery target.
9. If you met someone with an akita would they be riding a moped, exercising a dog, playing a computer game or wearing a tunic?
10. What are your phalanges?
11. Add a T to a skilled doctor to find a fish.
12. Sufferers of coeliac disease have to avoid eating which substance?
13. Is rhubarb a fruit or a vegetable?
14. In Australia what is the Fremantle Doctor?
15. If you arranged all the US states in alphabetical order which would come first and which would come last?
16. In Greek mythology, which princess said she would only marry the man who could beat her at running?

▬▬▬▬ ANSWERS ▬▬▬▬

1 Taste is partly a smell sensation, so when your nose is blocked food doesn't taste the same, 2 Balboa, 3 Procrastination, 4 Fetlar, 5 Greece, 6 Poland, 7 A military camp for training recruits, disciplining young offenders etc, 8 Gold, red, blue, black, white, 9 Exercising a Japanese breed of dog, 10 Bones in your fingers and toes, 11 Surgeon to sturgeon, 12 Gluten, 13 Botanically it's a vegetable, 14 An afternoon sea breeze, 15 Alabama and Wyoming, 16 Atalanta.

The SUNDAY POST
FAMILY
QUIZ BOOK

BRAINBOX
For smarties only!

1. Arch girder, cantilever, suspension, are all types of what?
2. What is measured by a galvanometer?
3. What is neoprene?
4. Sufferers of nosophobia fear strong smells, disease or strong winds?
5. Who was the first American in space?
6. An osteopath heals by massage, hypnotism or herbal medicine?
7. If the temperature is 68 degrees Fahrenheit, what is it in Centigrade?
8. What is the main constituent in the manufacture of glass?
9. What's the connection between dahlia, fuchsia and forsythia?
10. When dealing with computers, what is RSI?
11. Dendrology is the study of trees, teeth or barbed wire fence construction?
12. What is made using the Bessemer Process?
13. Is a decalitre a tenth of a litre, or a unit of ten litres?
14. Ag is the chemical symbol for what?
15. Was an autogiro a type of ship, car or aircraft?
16. For what purpose is an emetic administered?

ANSWERS

1 Bridges, 2 The flow of electric currents, 3 A synthetic rubber, 4 Disease, 5 John Glenn, 6 Massage (and manipulation), 7 20 degrees C, 8 Sand, 9 They are all plants named after people, 10 Repetitive Strain Injury – inflamed tissue caused by abnormally high use of muscle, tendon, or ligament, 11 Trees, 12 Steel, 13 A unit of ten litres (a decilitre is a tenth of a litre), 14 Silver, 15 Aircraft, 16 To induce vomiting.

SPORT
Actively awesome!

● 1-5 Relegation! ● 6-11 Mid-table! ● 12-16 Champions!

1. Who was golf's US Masters champion in 2007?
2. Name the four semi-finalists in the 2007 Cricket World Cup.
3. What nationality is the footballer Deco?
4. Who play their home matches at Bramall Lane?
5. Which of these is not a tennis Grand Slam venue? Wimbledon, Queen's Club or Flushing Meadow?
6. Who captained Celtic when they won the European Cup in 1967?
7. Where is the Cresta Run?
8. Where were football's 2004 European Championships held?
9. In which sport does Chris Hoy excel?
10. Which Rugby Union team are known as the Tigers?
11. From which club did Manchester United sign Wayne Rooney?
12. In which sport would you find the words 'side' and 'bias'?
13. Who finished runners-up to Celtic in the Scottish Premier League season 2006-2007?
14. Which British Grand Prix driver claimed a podium place in the first three races in 2007?
15. What does UEFA stand for?
16. Which horse won the 2007 Grand National?

GENERAL KNOWLEDGE

Take the test.

1. The name of which Hebridean island means Mountain of the Fords?
2. What was the first product to be advertised on UK commercial TV?
3. Which Charles Dickens novel features a character called Mealy Potatoes?
4. How many Prime Ministers served under Queen Victoria — 8, 9, 10 or 12?
5. Change the middle letter of a lochside town in central Scotland to find a Highland town with an RAF base.
6. Eva Braun is remembered for her friendship with which notorious figure?
7. Is a coatimundi a North American Indian head-dress, a racoon-like carnivore, a hot African wind or an Arctic mist?
8. What is the maximum speed limit allowed for a car towing either a trailer or a caravan on the motorway?
9. Unscramble HALF IN WATER to track down a familiar relation.
10. Name the young lion in the movie *The Lion King*.
11. How many players make up a Canadian Football side?
12. Where do bees usually carry collected pollen?
13. What was comedy actor Fatty Arbuckle's real first name — Roscoe, Hugo, Luigi or Laurence?
14. Who was said to have been struck blind when Lady Godiva rode through the streets of Coventry?
15. A nocturnal creature sleeps by day and comes out at night. What is an animal that sleeps at night and is up by day?
16. What do you call a group of kangaroos?

ANSWERS

15 Diurnal, 16 Mob or troop.
11 Twelve players, 12 In sacs on their hind legs, 13 Roscoe, 14 Peeping Tom,
6 Adolf Hitler, 7 A raccoon-like carnivore, 8 60 mph, 9 Father-in-law, 10 Simba,
1 Benbecula, 2 Gibbs SR toothpaste, 3 David Copperfield, 4 Ten, 5 Kinross to Kinloss,

THE SUNDAY POST
FAMILY
QUIZ BOOK

GENERAL KNOWLEDGE

Facts are fun!

1. In the popular song, what follows the following line? 'The hills are alive with the sound of music'.
2. Name three musical instruments beginning with TR.
3. Which creature lives in a lodge?
4. Name the world famous persona who visited Glasgow's Bellahouston Park in 1982.
5. Large golden arches on a roadside sign might tempt you to stop for what?
6. Pick the odd one out — Cooper, Taylor, Thatcher, McLaren, Smith or Baker?
7. Which brand of sportswear is also a South African gazelle?
8. Should a lobster have four, six or eight legs?
9. Trooping of the Colour in London takes place in what month of the year?
10. Is an Ulster a type of hat, overcoat, waistcoat or slipper?
11. Who was the first US president to resign from office?
12. Was Paul McCartney knighted in 1991, 1994 or 1997?
13. If you ordered bratwurst in a Berlin restaurant what would be brought to your table?
14. Are there four, five or six players in a curling team?
15. In *The Simpsons* cartoon what kind of animals are Itchy and Scratchy?
16. In days gone by how did a scrivener make his living?

ANSWERS

1 'With songs they have sung for a thousand years', 2 Trumpet, trombone, triangle, 3 A beaver, 4 Pope John Paul II, 5 A burger at McDonald's, 6 Mclaren is the only name that didn't originate in trades, 7 Reebok, 8 Eight, 9 June, 10 A long overcoat, 11 Richard Nixon in 1974, 12 1997, 13 A pork sausage, 14 Four, 15 A cat and mouse, 16 As a writer, clerk or scribe.

GENERAL KNOWLEDGE

Quite quizzical!

1. Beaulieu in Hampshire has a museum devoted to what?
2. Which everyday food item was the title of a 1980s BBC sitcom set in Liverpool?
3. Is the silver inset of a £2 coin larger or smaller than a 5p piece?
4. What percentage of a jellyfish is water — 65, 75, 85 or 95?
5. When does down soar up?
6. *The Cage* was the pilot episode of which long-running TV sci-fi series?
7. What is the true definition of the Japanese word tsunami?
8. We've all heard of IVF treatment, but what exactly do the letters stand for?
9. When did Coca-Cola first appear on the market — 1886, 1896, 1906 or 1916?
10. What was Buddy Holly's real name?
11. Why are people who take game illegally called poachers?
12. Was Arthur Ashe, Boris Becker or Jimmy Connors the first unseeded Wimbledon men's singles champion?
13 Which island was once known as Van Diemen's Land?
14. Singultus is more often known as — tennis elbow, hiccups, dandruff or athlete's foot?
15. Which part of a flower might remind you of a gun?
16. Name an Old Testament book that is named after a woman.

ANSWERS

1 Motor cars, 2 Bread, 3 Larger, 4 Around 95 per cent, 5 When it's on a duck, 6 Star Trek, 7 Harbour wave, 8 In vitro fertilization, 9 1886, 10 Charles Hardin Holley, 11 It's from the French pocher, meaning pocket, 12 Boris Becker, 13 Tasmania, 14 Hiccups, 15 The pistil, or seed producing, part, 16 Ruth or Esther.

KIDS' STUFF
Practically playtime!

1. What type of creature is a Red Admiral?
2. In which English city would you find the Bull Ring?
3. Which musical contains the song *Climb Ev'ry Mountain?*
4. What is the capital city of Austria?
5. What do you call a collection of lions?
6. Which giant was stopped in his tracks by a stone from David's sling?
7. Dundee stands at the mouth of which river?
8. Which language is spoken in Brazil? Spanish or Portuguese?
9. Which London landmark is named after an Egyptian queen?
10. What is the name of the young boy in Rudyard Kipling's *Jungle Book?*
11. His real name is Reg Dwight, but how do we know him?
12. Which football team are known as the Gunners?
13. In the nursery rhyme, where did Little Jack Horner sit?
14. Which two brothers front the pop group Oasis?
15. What was Thailand formerly known as?
16. Jerseys and Fresians are breeds of which animal?

ANSWERS

1 Butterfly, 2 Birmingham, 3 The Sound of Music, 4 Vienna, 5 A pride, 6 Goliath, 7 River Tay, 8 Portuguese, 9 Cleopatra's Needle, 10 Mowgli, 11 Elton John, 12 Arsenal, 13 In a corner, 14 Noel and Liam Gallacher, 15 Siam, 16 Cows.

ENTERTAINMENT
Are you a star solver?

1. He's been from *Pole to Pole* and gone *Full Circle* – what is his name?
2. Did William Shakespeare have any children?
3. What was Harpo Marx's proper name?
4. Basil, Sybil and Manuel featured in which classic TV comedy series?
5. An oboe has four strings – true or false?
6. Who wrote the novel *Last Of The Mohicans?*
7. How many miles to Babylon were there, according to the nursery rhyme?
8. What is the best hand in the game of Poker?
9. Mustard-seed, Peaseblossom, Cobweb, Moth – where would you find all these together?
10. Which ballet term means 'a dance for two'?
11. Charlie Dimmock, Alan Titchmarsh, Percy Thrower – what's the connection?
12. How many squares are there on a Scrabble board – 169, 196 or 225?
13. In the film of the same name, what kind of creature is *Stuart Little?*
14. In which TV soap would you find the Dingle family?
15. Name the superstar who called her daughter Chastity and her son Elijah Blue.
16. Was the Beatles' first hit record *Please Please Me!, Help!* or *Love Me Do!?*

ANSWERS

1 Michael Palin, 2 Yes – one son and two daughters, 3 Arthur, 4 Fawlty Towers, 5 False – it's a wind instrument, 6 James Fenimore Cooper, 7 Three score and ten, 8 A Royal Flush (ace to ten in the same suit), 9 In Shakespeare's Midsummer Night's Dream – they are fairy attendants of Titania, 10 Pas de Deux, 11 They all have been gardening experts on TV, 12 225, 13 A mouse, 14 Emmerdale, 15 Cher, 16 Love Me Do!

GENERAL KNOWLEDGE

How much do YOU know?

● 1-5 Know a little! ● 6-11 Know a lot! ● 12-16 Know it all!

1. Which comedian co-wrote the tongue-in-cheek book *Parliamo Glasgow* as a guide to speaking fluent Glaswegian?
2. Which country's flag features a blue Star of David in the centre?
3. Is a Rickenbacker a piano, drum or guitar?
4. From where do cars bearing the following international registration letters come: a) CH, b) ZA, c) J, d) NL?
5. Why does the American Flag have 13 stripes?
6. County Donegal is famous for which fabric?
7. Thomas Arne's most famous work is often heard at the Last Night Of The Proms. Name it.
8. If you are watching a bonspiel, what game is taking place?
9. Which actor made most *Tarzan* films — Lex Barker, Johnny Weissmuller, Gordon Scott, Ron Ely?
10. Flute, tulip, balloon and chimney are what?
11. You can find Fingal's Cave on which of Scotland's islands?
12. From whose head did William Tell allegedly shoot an apple?
13. Which cocktail consists of vodka, orange juice and Galliano liqueur?
14. Is a histogram used most often by a doctor, dentist, gardener, engineer or statistician?
15. Which two leaders cut the ribbons to open the Channel Tunnel in 1994?
16. Your GP has diagnosed varicella, so what's wrong?

ANSWERS

1 Stanley Baxter (along with Alex Mitchell), 2 Israel, 3 Guitar, 4 a) Switzerland, b) South Africa, c) Japan, d) Netherlands, 5 There were originally 13 states of the Union, 6 Tweed, 7 Rule Britannia, 8 Curling, 9 Johnny Weissmuller, 10 Drinking glasses, 11 Staffa, 12 His son's, 13 Harvey Wallbanger, 14 Statistician. It's a graph using rectangles of varying heights, 15 Queen Elizabeth II and President Mitterand, 16 You have chickenpox.

GENERAL KNOWLEDGE

Take the test.

1. What was the only takeaway food not to be rationed during World War Two?
2. Which alcoholic drink is mixed with grapefruit and lemon juice to make a Monkey Wrench cocktail?
3. When is a drinking glass acrobatic?
4. In which sea can the Strait of Messina be found?
5. Which Scottish castle did the BBC use to replicate *Colditz* in the TV series?
6. Creosote is wood preservative distilled from what?
7. Macaroni, gentoo and chinstrap are all types of which bird?
8. What is the name of the railway which runs from Moscow to Vladivostok?
9. According to the Christian calendar, what is the first day of Lent?
10. What does it mean if a meal is served 'a la russe'?
11. Add two letters to a red wine to make a woodwind instrument.
12. Do snakes blink?
13. The mirror image of a clock set at 1.30 would appear to read what time?
14. Which classic rock song contains the line, 'Thunderbolt and lightning very very frightening'?
15. In yoga, why is the lotus position so called?
16. What are tenterhooks?

ANSWERS

1 Fish and chips, 2 White rum, 3 When it's a tumbler, 4 The Mediterranean, 5 Stirling Castle, 6 Coal tar, 7 Penguin, 8 The Trans-Siberian Railway, 9 Ash Wednesday, 10 Courses are brought to the table one at a time in a set order, 11 Add IN to claret to make clarinet, 12 No, they don't have proper eyelids, 13 10.30, 14 Bohemian Rhapsody, by Queen, 15 It's said to represent a lotus flower floating on a pond, 16 Hooked nails for stretching cloth on a frame called a tenter.

SPORT

Actively awesome!

1. What in cricket is the popping-crease?
2. How many players are there in a basketball team?
3. On which race-course is the Oaks run?
4. What is the maximum age of a filly in horse-racing? Three, four or five years?
5. Cruiserweight was the original name for which present-day boxing weight?
6. Was Gordon Richards, who died in 1986, an athlete, jockey, golfer or footballer?
7. The Tokyo Olympics were held in what year?
8. In the game of golf, what do you call a score of two strokes under par for a hole?
9. When was the original Wembley Stadium completed – 1921, 1923 or 1925?
10. Name the man who became World Featherweight Boxing Champion in June 1985.
11. In which sport might you use a Red Hackle?
12. How many Wimbledon Singles finals did John McEnroe participate in?
13. What is the purpose of an aerofoil on a racing car?
14. What does the cricketing term 'off break' mean?
15. Which was the first British football club to use artificial turf as their playing surface?
16. True or false – golfer Bernhard Langer is Australian?

ANSWERS

1 It's the line limiting the batsman's position, 2 Five, 3 Epsom, 4 Four years, 5 Light heavy-weight, 6 Jockey, 7 1964, 8 Eagle, 9 1923, 10 Barry McGuigan, 11 Fishing, 12 Five, winning three and losing two, 13 It counters the 'lift' created by the highly-streamlined shape travelling at speed, 14 It's a ball that, on bowling, comes in towards the batsman from the off side, 15 Queens Park Rangers, 16 False. He is German.

GENERAL KNOWLEDGE
Facts are fun!

1. In which sport was Peter Nicol a champion?
2. According to the old saying, who do you need 'a lang spoon tae sup wi'?
3. Do your hand and wrist contain more bones than your foot and ankle?
4. If brothers are fraternal, what are sisters?
5. Name four commonly used words ending in 'dous'.
6. Which Scottish boy's name means 'hooked nose' — Angus, Cameron, Fraser or Duncan?
7. When you stop smoking how long is it before your body is free of nicotine?
8. What would you expect to find in an oast-house?
9. What would a jeweller mean by the collet?
10. Which is America's 'Treasure' state — Montana, Missouri or Maryland?
11. How many players are there in a volleyball team?
12. What can be a sponge, a notebook or an apartment?
13. To which family of birds does the magpie belong?
14. Which country is commonly believed to have the highest number of centenarians?
15. How did the pound sign originate?
16. Name three places in London with namesakes in New York.

ANSWERS

1 Squash, 2 A Fifer, 3 Yes, one more, 4 Sororal, 5 Tremendous, horrendous, stupendous and hazardous, 6 Cameron, 7 Two to four days, 8 Drying hops or malt for beer-making, 9 The part of a ring in which a stone is set, 10 Montana, 11 Six, 12 A pad, 13 The crow family, 14 Japan, 15 It's a stylised L, from the Latin libra, a pound, 16 Any three from Soho, Chelsea, Greenwich, Kew Gardens, Norwood, Broadway.

GENERAL KNOWLEDGE
Quite quizzical!

● 1-5 Quite quiet! ● 6-11 Quite qualified! ● 12-16 Quite quick!

1. If your birthday is in June is your birthstone pearl, ruby or emerald?
2. What would you use an anemometer for?
3. Queen Liliuokalani was the last queen of which Pacific island?
4. What did the US game 'beano' later become known as?
5. What are the two most common allergies?
6. Tia Maria, vodka and Coke are mixed to make what?
7. Euro banknotes come in seven denominations. What are they?
8. Which British department store claims it is 'never knowingly undersold'?
9. Unscramble WAVE GLOVE IN BED HUNT to recall a famous classical composer.
10. Can you think of three capital cities beginning and ending with the same letter?
11. Who wrote the music for the operetta, *The Merry Widow*?
12. Drop an E from the end of a luxury car to find a breed of cattle.
13. Why do we say going 'hell for leather' when doing our utmost to achieve something?
14. Which planet is nearest to the sun?
15. Solve these 'cor' words: a) long-necked diving sea bird, b) ceremonial crowning, c) abundant supply of good things, d) obese.
16. In which European country was tennis player Martina Navratilova born?

ANSWERS

1 Pearl, 2 To measure wind speed, 3 Hawaii, 4 Bingo — the cards were originally marked with beans, 5 Hay fever and dust mites, 6 A Black Russian, 7 5, 10, 20, 50, 100, 200 and 500, 8 John Lewis, 9 Ludwig van Beethoven, 10 Accra (Ghana), Ankara (Turkey), Oslo (Norway), Warsaw (Poland), Addis Ababa (Ethiopia), Abuja (Nigeria) etc, 11 Franz Lehar, 12 Limousine to Limousin, 13 It's a reference to a hard, fast or reckless horse ride on a leather saddle, 14 Mercury, 15 a) Cormorant, b) coronation, c) cornucopia, d) corpulent, 16 Czechoslovakia in 1956.

KIDS' STUFF
Young at heart!

● 1-5 Year one! ● 6-11 Year four! ● 12-16 Year seven!

1. Which author wrote the Famous Five series of adventures?
2. Who narrated the *Magic Roundabout* stories?
3. Which is the missing Spice Girl? Sporty, Posh, Baby, Ginger and____.
4. Which television show links the following presenters? John Noakes, Peter Duncan and Connie Huq.
5. Are the pop group Arctic Monkeys from Scotland, England or Wales?
6. Who played the part of Hagrid in the *Harry Potter* films?
7. Fill in the missing words. Great____of China, Hanging____of Babylon, Leaning Tower of____.
8. What was the second in the *Lord of the Rings* adventures?
9. Which town is further north? Newcastle or Liverpool?
10. What do you call a shape with eight sides? An octagon or an optagon?
11. Guernsey and Sark are part of which island group?
12. Which actor plays the title role in the *Mr Bean* movies?
13. In the nursery rhyme, what ran away with the spoon?
14. Emperor Gruumm, Mesogog and Divatix are all enemies of which group of super heroes?
15. Where in Britain would you find Legoland?
16. What are the surnames of TV personalities Ant and Dec?

ANSWERS

1 Enid Blyton, 2 Eric Thomson, 3 Scary, 4 Blue Peter, 5 Scotland, 6 Robbie Coltrane, 7 Wall, Gardens, Pisa, 8 The Two Towers, 9 Newcastle, 10 Octagon, 11 Channel Islands, 12 Rowan Atkinson, 13 The dish, 14 Power Rangers, 15 Windsor, 16 McPartlin and Donnelly.

BRAINBOX

For smarties only!

1. 'He' is the chemical symbol for which element?
2. Tectonics is the study of the movement of what on the Earth's surface?
3. Your backbone is a flexible chain of how many bones?
4. In psychiatry, ochlophobia is a fear of what?
5. Where in the human body would you find a stirrup?
6. When was Pluto discovered – 1910, 1920 or 1930?
7. An anemometer measures what?
8. Is a metamata a species of vegetable, a South American volcano, or a turtle?
9. How many eyes does a bee have?
10. Referring to plants, what does 'phototropic' mean?
11. How many chromosomes are there in a normal human body cell?
12. In what year did the Russians land a remote-control vehicle, Lunokhod, on the moon?
13. What is the purpose of a spectroscope?
14. Crohn's Disease affects which part of the body?
15. Which part of the eye determines its colour?
16. What is a young grouse called?

ANSWERS

1 Helium, 2 Rocks, 3 26, 4 Crowds, 5 It's a small bone in your ear, 6 1930, 7 Wind speed, 8 A turtle, 9 Five, 10 Responding to the direction from which light falls, 11 46, 12 1970, 13 It separates a light source into its different coloured components, 14 The small intestine, 15 The iris, 16 Poult.

GENERAL KNOWLEDGE

How much do YOU know?

● 1-5 Know a little! ● 6-11 Know a lot! ● 12-16 Know it all!

1. Was Tony Blair born before or after the beginning of the Queen's reign?
2. What is the lunula on your hand?
3. Which US TV series involved the residents of Walnut Grove?
4. If you're presbyopic what are you?
5. What does 'nether' mean in Netherlands?
6. Prospective students need to fill out an UCAS form. What does it stand for?
7. Which district of London is said to have taken its name from a huntsman's cry?
8. Explain the origin of the word goodbye.
9. Is Jupiter's beard something you would gaze at through a telescope, plant in your garden, consult your doctor about or install on your computer?
10. Which bird has the widest wingspan?
11. Which film won more Academy Awards — *Ben Hur* or *Titanic?*
12. What are the correct names for your upper and lower jawbones?
13. Who wrote the novel *Brighton Rock?*
14. In a famous film, how was John Merrick better known?
15. What is the main component in eggshell?
16. What would a doctor mean by the letters NYD?

ANSWERS

1 After. He was born in 1953, a year after the Queen came to the throne, 2 The white crescent-shape at the base of your fingernail, 3 Little House On The Prairie, 4 Long-sighted, 5 Lower, 6 Universities And Colleges Admissions Service, 7 Soho, 8 It's a derivation of 'God be with you', 9 Plant it in your garden – it's a flowering perennial, 10 The albatross, 11 Neither — both won 11 awards, 12 Maxilla and mandible, 13 Graham Greene, 14 The Elephant Man, 15 Calcium, 16 Not yet diagnosed.

THE SUNDAY POST
FAMILY
QUIZ BOOK

ENTERTAINMENT

Test your celebrity rating.

1. The 1960 film *Village of the Damned* was an adaptation of which John Wyndham novel?
2. Buster Crabbe played which early superhero in films of the 1930s?
3. Which 'numerical' band had a No.1 hit with *Never Had a Dream Come True* in December 2000?
4. How were John E Bartholomew and Ernest Wiseman better known to TV viewers?
5. Who first took over from Richard Whiteley as presenter of *Countdown?*
6. Name the youngest family member in TV's *The Simpsons.*
7. Where are 'Bollywood' films made?
8. Julie Andrews won an Oscar for which 1964 musical?
9. Which ex-supermodel was once married to actor Richard Gere?
10. In which fictional village is radio's *The Archers* set?
11. Which pop star appeared in the title role of the movie *Merry Christmas, Mr Lawrence?*
12. Which actress played the overpowering boss in the film adaptation of *The Devil Wears Prada?*
13. Butterfly McQueen played which role in the epic film *Gone With the Wind?*
14. She's had several husbands, but what was *Coronation Street's* Deirdre Barlow's maiden name?
15. The song *Big Spender* comes from which musical that opened on Broadway in 1966?
16. Who was the original presenter of TV's *Ready, Steady, Cook?*

ANSWERS

1 *The Midwich Cuckoos,* 2 Flash Gordon, 3 S Club 7, 4 Morecambe and Wise, 5 Des Lynam, 6 Maggie, 7 Mumbai, India, 8 Mary Poppins, 9 Cindy Crawford, 10 Ambridge, 11 David Bowie, 12 Meryl Streep, 13 Prissy the maid, 14 Hunt, 15 *Sweet Charity,* 16 Fern Britten.

GENERAL KNOWLEDGE

Take the test.

1. How many children were there in TV's *The Waltons?*
2. How many are in a myriad?
3. Where would you find a MacPherson strut?
4. Was Florence Nightingale alive at the time of World War One?
5. When you hesitate about something you 'shilly-shally'. Why?
6. Unscramble NICE SALT WORDS to locate a famous Royal residence.
7. Which member of the cat family is also known as the hunting leopard?
8. If a French wine is described as doux, is it medium dry or medium sweet?
9. Why should a pteronophobic person not keep pet canaries?
10. In Morse Code, which letter is represented by four dots — F, H, J or L?
11. What are court cards in a pack of cards?
12. What was wampum to a Native North American?
13. Is a seahorse a fish?
14. How many stomachs do ants have?
15. Is a pulsar something mostly of interest to a chef, a surgeon, an astronomer or a motor mechanic?
16. Who or what were the Mau Mau?

ANSWERS

1 Seven, John-Boy, Mary-Ellen, Jason, Ben, Erin, Jim-Bob and Elizabeth, 2 An infinite number, though originally it meant 10,000, 3 Under a car – it's part of the suspension, 4 No, she died in 1910, 5 It's a corruption of 'will, I, shall I?', 6 Windsor Castle, 7 The cheetah, 8 Medium sweet, 9 They have a fear of feathers, 10 The letter H, 11 The kings, queens and jacks, 12 Bead or shell necklaces, belts etc used as currency for bartering, 13 Yes, 14 Two, 15 Astronomer – it's a star, 16 A secret political society of Kikuyu tribesmen formed in 1952 to drive Europeans out of Kenya.

SPORT
Fit and healthy!

1. Foil, sabre and epee are used in which sport?
2. Was Pele, the ex-Brazilian footballer, born in 1940, 1942 or 1944?
3. What is the number to the immediate left of the 3 on a dart board?
4. In bowls, what is the name for the white ball?
5. Which English football team plays its home games at Upton Park?
6. In what sport do teams compete for the Calcutta Cup — golf, rugby or cricket?
7. What are the colours of the rings on the Olympic Flag?
8. Which sport would you be taking part in if you entered a Canadian Pairs race?
9. In Badminton, what is the name of the line parallel to, and nearest to, the net?
10. Was Evonne Goolagong a female cricketer, short-distance runner or tennis player?
11. What is the minimum number of darts possible for a 301 finish?
12. What sport do you associate with a player called Tuigamala?
13. In golf, what was a 'baffy'?
14. Which English football team are known as the Foxes?
15. Who partnered Martina Navratilova in the 1979 Wimbledon Ladies' Doubles Final?
16. In which sport are competitors not allowed to play left-handed — polo or croquet?

ANSWERS

1 Fencing, 2 1940, 3 19, 4 Jack, 5 West Ham United. It's England v Scotland, 7 Black, blue, red, green, yellow, 8 Canoeing, 9 Short service line, 10 Tennis player, 11 Six, 12 Rugby League, 13 A wooden-shafted five wood, 14 Leicester City, 15 Billie Jean King, 16 Polo.

GENERAL KNOWLEDGE

Facts are fun!

1. How many paintings did Vincent Van Gogh sell during his lifetime? One, two or none?
2. Which is Britain's oldest university?
3. The name Pinocchio derives from the Italian for — pine seed, wooden boy, puppet boy or pine puppet?
4. Name the smallest US state.
5. Which team scored the first goal in the 2002 World Cup finals in France?
6. Name Scottish football's national stadium.
7. Unscramble A DEER LUG O JOY I to reveal a *Coronation Street* legend.
8. What type of tree is, reputedly, the UK's tallest?
9. When the moon is waxing does it appear to be growing or decreasing in size?
10. How many monarchs have we had since Queen Victoria?
11. If cattle are bovine, what are sheep?
12. How many US states have land borders with Canada?
13. A jeroboam holds how many standard sized bottles of champagne?
14. The Great Dark Spot is a feature of — Mars, Venus, Neptune or Uranus?
15. Which popular cartoon family lived in Bedrock?
16. Which car was known as the tin snail?

ANSWERS

1 Just one, Red Vineyard at Arles, 2 Oxford, 3 Pine seed, 4 Rhode Island, 5 Senegal, 6 Hampden Park, 7 Julie Goodyear, 8 A Douglas fir near Dunkeld, 9 Growing, 10 Five – Edward VII, George V, Edward VIII, George VI, Elizabeth II, 11 Ovine, 12 Ten – Washington, Idaho, Montana, North Dakota, Minnesota, New York, Vermont, New Hampshire, Maine, Alaska, 13 Four, 14 Neptune, 15 The Flintstones, 16 Citroen 2CV.

GENERAL KNOWLEDGE
Quite quizzical!

● 1-5 Quite quiet! ● 6-11 Quite qualified! ● 12-16 Quite quick!

1. What is the most common first name in the world?
2. Pick the odd one out from these five Martial arts — sumo, kung fu, kendo, aikido, judo.
3. Which is the most sparsely populated country in Europe?
4. What kind of entertainer might have MIMC after their name?
5. Which US president was nearly President Blythe?
6. Which Scottish town was formerly known as Aberbrothock?
7. In movies, who was Fransisco Scaramanga?
8. Give the modern names for the country formerly called Abyssinia.
9. When Peter Parker dons a costume he becomes which comic book hero?
10. Rhona Martin made her name by playing which sport?
11. Who normally makes the first speech at a wedding reception?
12. How many types of grape can be used to make true champagne?
13. Rearrange HOT JOKER to recall a TV character portrayed by William Shatner.
14. Identify the following sports — grasshopper-like insect, timber garden borders, popular sweet with a hole, squeeze tightly.
15. What's unusual about a plant grown hydroponically?
16. Bharat is the ancient name of which former British colony?

ANSWERS

1 Mohammed, 2 Kung fu is Chinese in origin, the others are Japanese, 3 Iceland, 4 A magician. It stands for Member of the Inner Magic Circle, 5 Bill Clinton. Born William Jefferson Blythe, he took his stepfather's name at 15, 6 Arbroath, 7 A villain in the James Bond movie The Man With The Golden Gun, 8 Ethiopia, 9 Spiderman, 10 Curling. She's an Olympic gold medalist, 11 The bride's father, 12 Three — Chardonnay, Pinot Meunier and Pinot Noir, 13 TJ Hooker, 14 Cricket, fencing, polo, squash, 15 It's grown in water without soil, 16 It's the Hindi name for India.

GENERAL KNOWLEDGE
How much do YOU know?

● 1-5 Know a little! ● 6-11 Know a lot! ● 12-16 Know it all!

1. 'Walking through an empty house, tears in my eyes,' are lyrics from which well-known Abba song?
2. In which decade did the UK last have a coalition government?
3. 'Let not the deep swallow me up' is a motto inscribed around medals awarded for gallantry by which organisation?
4. What is 'Big Brum' in Birmingham?
5. How many years make up a wooden wedding anniversary?
6. Solve the following 'chain' clues: a) shackled prisoners, b) order of seniority, c) mail received by many.
7. Is a sockeye a bird, mammal, fish or reptile?
8. On which island could you visit the city of Heraklion?
9. When was the first Wimbledon tennis tournament — 1855, 1866, 1877 or 1888?
10. Which is further south — the northern tip of mainland Orkney or the southern tip of mainland Shetland?
11. Unscramble WE ALL BANK JOE to find a female TV personality.
12. How many players are in a water polo team?
13. The population of the world is more than three, four, five or six billion?
14. What's the English equivalent of a Scottish laird?
15. If you ordered a manzanilla in a Spanish bar, what would you receive?
16. LBA is the code for which English airport?

ANSWERS

1 Knowing Me, Knowing You, 2 The 1940s, under Winston Churchill during the war, 3 The RNLI, 4 The clock tower of Birmingham Museum and Art Gallery, 5 Five, 6 a) chain gang, b) chain of command, c) chain letter, 7 Fish – it's a salmon, 8 Crete, 9 1877, 10 The northern tip of mainland Orkney, 11 Joan Bakewell, 12 Seven, 13 More than six billion, 14 A squire, 15 A dry, pale sherry, 16 Leeds Bradford Airport.

ENTERTAINMENT

Are you a star solver?

1. What is the name of the local newspaper in the TV soap *EastEnders?*
2. Who are Yum-Yum and Nanki-Poo?
3. In the film *Bambi,* is the animal called Flower an elephant, deer or skunk?
4. In which fictional town is TV's *Casualty* set?
5. Which legendary entertainer was called Satchmo?
6. Who is the target for assassination in the book *The Day Of The Jackal?*
7. What would you do with a clarsach?
8. Was Stan Laurel the thin half or the fat half of the comedy partnership, Laurel and Hardy?
9. In which card game would you 'stick'?
10. The 1970s series *Howard's Way* was set in what location?
11. According to poet Robert Burns, where does 'a body meet a body'?
12. Harrison Ford played what part in the film *Blade Runner?*
13. Who wrote *The Great Gatsby* and *Tender Is The Night?*
14. Whose epitaph was 'On the whole, I'd rather be in Philadelphia'?
15. Who played Baldrick in TV's classic comedy, the *Blackadder* series?
16. When did Kylie Minogue take *I Should Be So Lucky* to the top of the charts?

ANSWERS

1 The *Walford Gazette,* 2 The two lovers in *The Mikado,* 3 A skunk, 4 Holby, 5 Louis Armstrong, 6 General De Gaulle, of France, 7 Play it – it's a musical instrument like a harp, 8 The thin half, 9 *Pontoon,* 10 A boatyard, 11 *Comin' Through The Rye,* 12 He played an ex-cop who terminates replicants, 13 F Scott Fitzgerald, 14 WC Fields, 15 Tony Robinson, 16 January 1988.

GENERAL KNOWLEDGE

Take the test.

1. Who advertised his mail order course with the slogan, 'I was a seven stone weakling'?
2. If someone gave you a Bath Oliver what would you do with it?
3. Why is *The Deathly Hallows* of interest to thousands of youngsters?
4. Unscramble ATHENIAN LOCAL DANCE to find a well-known Scottish waterway.
5. Andrew Motion is the holder of which prestigious title?
6. Which TV soap opens with an aerial view of the Millennium Dome?
7. What is partan bree?
8. Benny was a popular character in a woolly hat in which former TV soap opera?
9. Is a baobab a woodwind instrument, a fruit tree, a lizard or a jacket?
10. Who is 'the Beast of Bolsover'?
11. How is Edson Arantes do Nascimento better known?
12. The peach tree is a member of which family of plants — rose, cactus, heath or mallow?
13. Which is America's 'Beehive' state — Tennessee, Michigan or Utah?
14. Name the nations which take part in Rugby Union's Six Nations Tournament.
15. Who played Cockney spiv Flash Harry in the *St Trinian's* films?
16. What is your solar plexus?

ANSWERS

1 Body-builder Charles Atlas, 2 Eat it — it's the title of JK Rowling's final Harry Potter novel, 4 The Caledonian Canal, 5 Poet Laureate, 6 EastEnders, 7 Crab soup, 8 Crossroads, 9 It's a fruit tree, 10 It's a nickname for politician Dennis Skinner, 11 As former Brazilian footballer Pele, 12 The rose family, 13 Utah, 14 Scotland, England, Ireland, Wales, France and Italy, 15 George Cole, 16 It's a network of nerves in your abdomen.

The SUNDAY POST FAMILY QUIZ BOOK

GENERAL KNOWLEDGE

Facts are fun!

● 1-5 Could improve! ● 6-11 Getting better! ● 12-16 The best!

1. *By The Sleepy Lagoon* is the theme tune to which popular radio programme?
2. Seen in a garden, what's a James Grieve?
3. Unscramble SCHOOLMASTER to reveal a seat of learning.
4. Hoist, fly and canton are all parts of what?
5. Flying into Marco Polo Airport, are you arriving in Vienna, Venice or Valletta?
6. Which house plant is often called the cast iron plant?
7. What was Prime Minister Sir Winston Churchill's full name?
8. How did the expression 'can't get a word in edgeways' originate?
9. British astronomers call it The Plough, but how do Americans refer to it?
10. In TV's *Thunderbirds* whose car is FAB1?
11. Could you have watched a cigarette advert on TV when Sir Edward Heath was Prime Minister?
12. What is the full title of the BNFL company?
13. Which young bird sounds like a kind of ring?
14. Why was golf once banned in Scotland?
15. At which battle did Davy Crockett die?
16. How is solid carbon dioxide also known?

ANSWERS

1 Desert Island Discs, 2 A variety of apple, 3 The classroom, 4 A flag, 5 Venice, 6 The aspidistra, because it's able to withstand neglect, 7 Winston Leonard Spencer Churchill, 8 From proof readers trying to squeeze in missing words in printed text, 9 The Big Dipper, 10 Lady Penelope's, 11 No, they were banned in 1965. Heath was PM from 1970-74, 12 British Nuclear Fuels Ltd, 13 A cygnet and a signet ring, 14 King James II believed it was interfering with archery practice, 15 The Alamo in 1836, 16 Dry ice.

SPORT

Play a part!

● 1-5 Solo player! ● 6-11 One of the gang! ● 12-16 Team captain!

1. What is the playing time in basketball matches?
2. Which country won the 1934 Football World Cup? France or Italy?
3. In baseball, what is the main area of play called?
4. What do all links golf courses have in common?
5. What was the name of Manchester City's previous ground?
6. Which snooker star is known as The Rocket?
7. True or false – Dunfermline FC play at West End Park?
8. The Rowley Mile can be found on which racecourse?
9. Racing driver Jim Clark was killed on which motor-racing circuit?
10. The terms 'gully', 'third man' and 'long-on' are used in which sport?
11. In the game of pool, what is the colour of the cue ball?
12. Does the team, Boston Red Sox, play baseball, American Football or ice hockey?
13. In what year did Seve Ballesteros first win the Open Golf Championship?
14. Which horse won the Grand National in 2000? Papillon, Butterfly or Caterpillar?
15. Bonspiel, rink, house, are all terms used in which sport?
16. David Ginola is a well-known name in the world of golf, football or athletics?

ANSWERS

1 Sixty minutes with three intervals, 2 Italy, 3 The diamond, 4 They are all beside the sea, 5 Maine Road, 6 Ronnie O'Sullivan, 7 False. They play at East End Park, 8 Newmarket, 9 Hockenheim, 10 Cricket, 11 White, 12 Baseball, 13 1979, 14 Papillon, 15 Curling, 16 Football.

GENERAL KNOWLEDGE

Quite quizzical!

1. What's the connection between *Mary Had A Little Lamb* and Thomas Edison?
2. What's unusual about the word queueing?
3. What's the basic difference between hunting and dress tartans?
4. Rearrange HOW I TABLE A REAL MOTIONS WIN to find a TV quiz show.
5. From where does TV soccer pundit Alan Hansen hail — Ayr, Alloa or Airdrie?
6. What are cookies on the Internet?
7. Is angelica something you'd see in an aquarium, a church, a hospital or a garden?
8. The Spanish word for war gives its name to what kind of soldier?
9. Which part of your body might be affected by rhinitis?
10. What kind of wolf got its name because it's normally found in forests?
11. Mary Arden was the mother of which famous person?
12. How did Welshman Reginald Truscott-Jones find fame in Hollywood?
13. During the 1960s who sang with the Dakotas?
14. What are Golden Globes?
15. Is a minke something you'd find in a garden centre, a baker's shop, the ocean or an orchestra?
16. Where is your radius bone?

ANSWERS

1 It was the rhyme he recited on the first recording of a human voice, 2 It contains five vowels in a row, 3 Hunting tartans use more subdued colours, 4 Who Wants To Be A Millionaire, 5 Alloa, Clackmannanshire, 6 Mechanisms that allow a web site to record visits and speed up future access, 7 A garden. It's a type of herb, 8 Guerrillas, from guerra (war), 9 Your nose, 10 The timber wolf, 11 William Shakespeare, 12 As actor Ray Milland, 13 Billy J Kramer, 14 American film and TV awards, 15 The ocean — it's a species of whale, 16 It's the outer of the two bones in the forearm.

GENERAL KNOWLEDGE
How much do YOU know?

● 1-5 Know a little! ● 6-11 Know a lot! ● 12-16 Know it all!

1. Name two towns or villages you would find if you were touring in The Trossachs.
2. Which are more fattening — boiled potatoes or chips?
3. In which famous American battle was General Antonio Lopez de Santa Anna the victor?
4. How many digits are there in a credit card number?
5. Where was ex-Labour leader, John Smith, buried?
6. Which lies further south — Isle of Wight or Isles of Scilly?
7. 'Oh, for the crags that are wild and majestic' wrote Lord Byron. But about which Scottish mountain?
8. Name two senior Scottish football teams with two 'U's in their name.
9. Which is the most popular curry dish served in UK Indian restaurants?
10. Monstera deliciosa is a plant more commonly known as what?
11. Aspen, Meribel and Cortina are all famous for what?
12. Income Tax was first introduced in this country to help pay for a war. Against whom — the Boers, Hitler or Napoleon?
13. Which sign of the Zodiac covers Christmas and the New Year?
14. Can you really hear better when it's dark?
15. Which female string quartet might make you think of 007?
16. When did Margaret Thatcher's son Mark become lost in the Sahara Desert – 1980, 1982 or 1984?

ANSWERS

1 Aberfoyle, Balquhidder, Callander, Doune etc, 2 Chips, especially when thinly cut, 3 The Alamo, 4 Sixteen, 5 On the island of Iona, 6 The Isles of Scilly, 7 Lochnagar, 8 Dundee United, Queen of the South or Stenhousemuir, 9 Chicken tikka masala, 10 Swiss cheese plant, 11 They're ski resorts, 12 Napoleon, 13 Capricorn, 14 No, but it often seems that way because there is less to distract you, 15 Bond, 16 1982.

GENERAL KNOWLEDGE

Take the test.

1. Who devised the package tour holiday — Billy Butlin, Fred Pontin or Thomas Cook?
2. How many grandchildren does the Queen have?
3. Issur Danielovitch Demsky found fame in Hollywood when he changed his name to what?
4. In the phonetic alphabet what word describes G?
5. Which is the most easterly African country — Egypt, Ethiopia, Kenya or Somalia?
6. Was Donald Duck originally called Dougal Duck, Donald Drake, Danny Duck or Ducky Duck?
7. What or who is Omerta?
8. Name two English racecourses beginning with New.
9. Do fennel leaves taste of salt, pepper, onion or aniseed?
10. The character Harry Lime features in which movie?
11. What is cuckoo spit on plants?
12. How many spots are there, in total, on the three highest dominoes in a standard set?
13. Was it Gilbert or Sullivan who wrote the music?
14. What does a mechanic mean by PAS?
15. The Jets and the Sharks are rival gangs in which popular musical?
16. Why is a gentleman's hairdresser called a barber?

ANSWERS

1 Thomas Cook, 2 Seven, 3 Kirk Douglas, 4 Golf, 5 Somalia, 6 Donald Drake, 7 It's the Mafia code of conduct, 8 Newmarket, Newton Abbot, Newbury or Newcastle, 9 Aniseed, 10 The Third Man, 11 A frothy secretion left by the frog-hopper insect to protect its larvae, 12 Thirty-three, 13 Sullivan, 14 Power-assisted steering, 15 West Side Story, 16 From the Latin barba, a beard.

The SUNDAY POST
FAMILY
QUIZ BOOK

ENTERTAINMENT

Are you a star solver?

1. Who played the title role in the film *Carrie*, based on the Stephen King novel?
2. In which year was the first episode of *Coronation Street* broadcast – 1958, 1959 or 1960?
3. *Goat's Head Soup* was the title of an album by which band, back in 1973?
4. Who or what was Timmy, one of the stars in Enid Blyton's *Famous Five* books?
5. What's the name of the deepest singing voice?
6. Bungle, George and Zippy were characters in which children's TV programme?
7. What was the name of John Noakes's dog when he was a *Blue Peter* presenter?
8. Who is the wife of comedian Billy Connolly?
9. Who composed the *Brandenburg Concertos?*
10. Telly Savalas portrayed which television detective?
11. Dustin Hoffman won an Oscar for the film *Rain Man*. But was it in 1988,1989 or 1990?
12. Which country music singer in America made records at two Californian prisons?
13. How many husbands has actress Elizabeth Taylor had?
14. Which stringed musical instrument can be bass, acoustic, Spanish or electric?
15. Can you name all four of the children's favourites, the *Teletubbies?*
16. The play *Cat On A Hot Tin Roof* was written by whom?

ANSWERS

1 Sissy Spacek, 2 1960, 3 The Rolling Stones, 4 A dog, 5 Basso profundo, 6 Rainbow, 7 Shep, 8 Pamela Stephenson, 9 JS Bach, 10 Kojak, 11 1988, 12 Johnny Cash, 13 Seven husbands, eight marriages (Burton twice), 14 Guitar, 15 Tinky Winky, Laa-Laa, Dipsy and Po, 16 Tennessee Williams.

BRAINBOX

For smarties only!

1. In the human body, where is the patella?
2. What does 'aneroid' mean in the phrase aneroid barometer?
3. Hippophobia is the fear of zoos, horses or camels?
4. What is the most common metal in the Earth's crust?
5. What is an alternative name for the Chile Pine tree?
6. Is a nematode – a radioactive rod, a positive electron or a type of worm?
7. How many millilitres are there, approximately, to one pint?
8. An ohm is a measure of what?
9. Is a pedometer for measuring children's feet, distance walked, or the size of bicycles?
10. What was the name of the first spacecraft to fly past Mars in July 1965?
11. Quicksilver is more commonly known as what?
12. How many calories are there in 100g of Cheddar cheese?
13. C is the chemical symbol for which element - carbon, copper or chlorine?
14. Our body is full of leucocytes. What are they?
15. The troposphere is – a tropical storm, a spherical map, or the lowest layer of the atmosphere?
16. Linseed oil comes from which plant?

ANSWERS

1 It is the knee-cap, 2 Without liquid or fluid, 3 Horses, 4 Aluminium, 5 The Monkey Puzzle tree, 6 A type of worm, 7 568 ml, 8 Electrical resistance, 9 Distance walked, 10 Mariner 4, 11 Mercury, 12 Approx. 410 calories, 13 Carbon, 14 White blood cells, 15 Lowest layer of the atmosphere, 16 Flax.

GENERAL KNOWLEDGE

Facts are fun!

● 1-5 Could improve! ● 6-11 Getting better! ● 12-16 The best!

1. Where can you always find February before January?
2. What did the MG in MG cars originally stand for?
3. In days gone by, fruit and veg sellers were called costermongers. Why?
4. Arch, whorl, radial, loop and double loop are all types of what?
5. In which British city might you be able to admire the Clifton Suspension Bridge?
6. Where can you see the sailing ship Cutty Sark?
7. A BBC2 panel game contains the name of a 1970s punk band. What is it?
8. What is the state capital of New York?
9. The expression 'to cut and run' means a hasty departure. How did it originate?
10. In the Shakespeare play, who is the wife of Othello?
11. Identify these areas of Edinburgh: a) forenoon elevation, b) farm building weight.
12. Who shot Lee Harvey Oswald?
13. What is bouillabaisse on a French restaurant menu?
14. Name TV cook Fanny Craddock's long-suffering husband.
15. What very large lorry takes its name from the Hindu god, Jagannath?
16. What is a mahout?

ANSWERS

1 In a dictionary, 2 Morris Garages, 3 From coster, a type of apple, and monger, one who trades, 4 Fingerprint patterns, 5 Bristol, 6 Greenwich, London, 7 Never Mind The Buzzcocks, 8 Albany, 9 It's a naval expression. Ships leaving port often found it easier to cut mooring ropes rather than untie them before running with the wind, 10 Desdemona, 11 a) Morningside, b) Barnton, 12 Jack Ruby, 13 A fish soup, 14 Johnny, 15 A juggernaut, 16 An elephant keeper.

GENERAL KNOWLEDGE

Quite quizzical!

1. The Apollo 11 astronauts left a plaque on the moon. It bears the names of how many men?
2. Which Australian opera singer has a toast named after her?
3. In what year did the UK switch to decimal currency?
4. Thomas Sullivan invented what — teabags, coffee, lemonade or Lucozade?
5. Bottlenose and common are species of which cute creature?
6. Which American state is abbreviated to MO?
7. In what year did Walt Disney's *Pinocchio* have its world premiere — 1935, 1940, 1955, 1960?
8. House dust consists mainly of what?
9. How is a sheet of paper measuring 420mm by 297mm commonly known?
10. What is the gaffer on a film set?
11. Name four of the six founder members of the European Economic Community.
12. Which dog is known as the King of Terriers?
13. Which European car manufacturer's name is Latin for 'let it be done'?
14. Do trees ever reach their full height or do they keep growing?
15. Which 1960s singer was famous for singing barefoot?
16. How many Sundays should there be in Advent?

ANSWERS

1 Four. Neil Armstrong, Edwin Aldrin, Michael Collins and President Nixon, 2 Dame Nellie Melba, 3 1971, 4 Teabags in 1904, 5 Dolphins, 6 Missouri, 7 1940, 8 Dead skin particles, 9 A3, 10 The chief electrician, 11 Any four from Belgium, France, West Germany, Italy, Luxembourg and the Netherlands, 12 The Airedale Terrier, 13 Fiat, 14 They keep growing new shoots until they die, 15 Sandie Shaw, 16 Four.

GENERAL KNOWLEDGE

How much do YOU know?

1. Who's had more British No.1 hits — Elvis or Cliff?
2. What was the purpose of Operation Desert Storm in 1991?
3. Which medical problem is derived from jeune, the French for yellow?
4. Name the films which featured these songs: a) *Take My Breath Away*, b) *Circle Of Life*, c) *It's Raining Men*.
5. Who was the first Prime Minister to use Chequers as a country retreat?
6. Who won the first Miss World Contest in 1951 — Miss Sweden, Miss Germany or Miss USA?
7. What is the fastest racket sport?
8. What makes naturally curly hair curly?
9. Tigh na Bruaich is a popular name for private houses and guesthouses in rural Scotland. What does it mean in English?
10. Which storybook characters live in the Hundred Acre Wood?
11. To which family of birds does the canary belong?
12. If you ordered pandowdy in an American restaurant what would you receive?
13. Is a woolly bear larger or smaller than a domestic cat?
14. How old was footballer Denis Law when he made his international debut for Scotland in 1958 — 17, 18 or 19?
15. In Edward Lear's *The Owl And The Pussycat* who married them?
16. How many bones are there in your hand and wrist?

ANSWERS

1 Elvis 17, Cliff 14, 2 To expel Iraqi invaders from Kuwait, 3 Jaundice, 4 a) Top Gun, b) The Lion King, c) Bridget Jones's Diary. 5 David Lloyd George in 1921, 6 Miss Sweden (Kiki Haakonson), 7 Pelota vasca, a Basque game where players have a wicker basket strapped to their arm, 8 Curly hair grows from curved follicles, while straight hair follicles are round, 9 House on the bank or hill, 10 Winnie The Pooh and friends, 11 The finch family, 12 A spiced apple pudding, 13 Smaller – it's a moth caterpillar, 14 18, 15 The turkey who lives on the hill, 16 27.

ENTERTAINMENT
Test your celebrity rating.

1. Which Hollywood actress gave her name to a lifejacket?
2. Who joined Elton John for the 1976 hit *Don't Go Breaking My Heart?*
3. Name four films with birds in their titles.
4. Which TV drama featured a character called Golly?
5. Name Lulu's joint-winning 1969 Eurovision Song Contest entry.
6. Name the four ghosts in Dickens' *A Christmas Carol.*
7. Which colour do actors consider to be unlucky on stage?
8. Name the type of vehicle which starred in the film, *Speed.*
9. Which *Good Life* actress later went *Solo?*
10. Who recorded the first No.1 record in the British pop chart - Elvis Presley, Johnny Mathis, Al Martino or Frank Sinatra?
11. Name the dog that looks after the Darling children in *Peter Pan.*
12. Pussy Galore was a character in which James Bond film?
13. Who created the melancholic minister known as The Rev IM Jolly?
14. Abba took *Knowing Me, Knowing You* to the No.1 spot in which year?
15. What was the second of the *Star Wars* films called?
16. Identify these Beatles hits: a) written on a gift tag, b) JK Rowling perhaps, c) brightly-coloured streamlined warship, d) titled pop star.

ANSWERS

1 Mae West, 2 Kiki Dee, 3 One Flew Over The Cuckoo's Nest, The Eagle Has Landed, The Raven, The Birds, Grey Owl, Robin Hood etc, 4 Monarch Of The Glen, played by Alexander Morton, 5 Boom-Bang-A-Bang, 6 Jacob Marley, The Ghost Of Christmas Past, The Ghost Of Christmas Present and The Ghost of Christmas Yet To Come, 7 Green, 8 A bus, 9 Felicity Kendal, 10 Al Martino with Here in My Heart in 1952, 11 Nana, 12 Goldfinger, 13 Rikki Fulton, 14 1977, 15 The Empire Strikes Back, 16 a) From Me To You, b) Paperback Writer, c) Yellow Submarine, d) Lady Madonna.

KIDS' STUFF
Practically playtime!

1. What do you fear if you suffer from vertigo?
2. Who marched his men to the top of the hill and marched them down again?
3. What's the difference between a stalactite and a stalagmite?
4. Which of the following is not a state in Australia? Victoria, Perth, Queensland or New South Wales?
5. What was Sir Francis Drake's ship called? The Golden Hind or the Silver Swan?
6. Do you find penguins living at the North Pole or at the South Pole?
7. On which Scottish island would you find the Cuillin Hills?
8. In which city does Aston Villa play home games?
9. Who is the patron saint of Wales?
10. In which two cities would you find the Millennium Stadium and Wembley Stadium?
11. In which direction does a Bishop move on a chessboard?
12. Urquhart Castle lies on the banks of which loch?
13. The Duke of Wellington finally defeated Napoleon at which battle in 1815?
14. In which Dickens novel does a young boy ask for more?
15. In which year will London host the Olympic games? 2010, 2012 or 2014?
16. What is the national emblem of Ireland?

ANSWERS

1 Heights, 2 The Grand Old Duke of York, 3 A stalactite grows down, a stalagmite grows up, 4 Perth. It is a city in Western Australia, 5 The Golden Hind, 6 South Pole, 7 Skye, 8 Birmingham, 9 Saint David, 10 Cardiff and London, 11 Diagonally, 12 Loch Ness, 13 Waterloo, 14 Oliver Twist, 15 2012, 16 Shamrock.

SPORT
Play a part!

● 1-5 Solo player! ● 6-11 One of the gang! ● 12-16 Team captain!

1. What colour of jersey does the leader wear in the Tour De France?
2. How many oarsmen compete in the Oxford/Cambridge University boat race?
3. What word describes the tennis stroke where the ball is returned before it bounces?
4. When was the first time women players received the same prize money as men at Wimbledon?
5. The Chair is the highest jump in which famous horse race?
6. In the world of football, who was The Doc?
7. With which sport do you associate the name Bernie Ecclestone?
8. Name three sports where the competitors travel backwards.
9. Who compete for the Curtis Cup?
10. What would you do on a dojo?
11. How many times did Graham Hill win the Monaco Grand Prix - three, four or five times?
12. In cricket, what is a 'googly'?
13. How many holes are there in a ten-pin bowling ball?
14. The World Amateur Snooker Championship was first held in which year?
15. Which English football team plays home games at The New Den?
16. Which sport uses the term 'spike'?

ANSWERS

1 Yellow, 2 Sixteen (two teams of eight), 3 Volley, 4 2007, 5 The Grand National, 6 Tommy Docherty, 7 Formula One Racing, 8 Rowing, tug of war and backstroke swimming, 9 Women amateur golfers from the United States and Great Britain and Ireland, 10 Practice judo. It's a kind of mat, 11 5 times, 12 A ball bowled to bounce in an unexpected direction, 13 Three, 14 1963, 15 Millwall, 16 Volleyball.

The SUNDAY POST FAMILY QUIZ BOOK

GENERAL KNOWLEDGE

Facts are fun!

1. In 1987 weatherman Michael Fish made a forecast he'll never be allowed to forget. Why?
2. How many players are there in a hurling side — 9, 11, 13 or 15?
3. Is a frogmouth a fish, a poisonous flower, a bird or a musical instrument?
4. What did George Eastman invent in the 1880s?
5. Is Bismark the state capital of North or South Dakota?
6. How did your Adam's apple get its name?
7. Suomi is the name of which country in its own language?
8. Who was the mother of King Edward VI of England?
9. What does ISBN on a book jacket stand for?
10. If someone gave you a luckenbooth would you pin it on your clothes, hang it on your wall, spread it and eat it or pluck its strings?
11. Why is someone who cheats you out of your money called a con man?
12. Is AUS the international car index mark for Austria or Australia?
13. In judo and karate, what colour belt marks a level of proficiency below a black belt?
14. Goat, osier and crack are types of what tree?
15. Name the fourth youngest of The Broon family who appear in *The Sunday Post* every week.
16. Who was movie star Marilyn Monroe's third husband?

ANSWERS

1 He said there would be no hurricane, hours before southern England was hit. 2 15, 3 A bird, 4 The first Kodak camera and roll film, 5 North, 6 From the notion that a piece of the forbidden fruit became stuck in Adam's throat, 7 Finland, 8 Jane Seymour, 9 International Standard Book Number, 10 Pin it on your clothes, it's a heart-shaped Celtic brooch, 11 Because he wins your confidence then swindles you, 12 Australia, 13 Brown belt, 14 Willow, 15 Horace, 16 Arthur Miller.

THE SUNDAY POST
FAMILY
QUIZ BOOK

GENERAL KNOWLEDGE

Quite quizzical!

1. In cold weather why do your lips crack and split more than skin on other parts of you body?
2. Who was the first footballer to score 100 league goals in both Scotland and England?
3. Who was the last British Prime Minister to return to office after losing a general election?
4. Unscramble I AGED TULIP CREATOR to discover a popular British actress.
5. Which is the most easterly Irish county?
6. What is Popocatepetl in Mexico?
7. Name the largest living mammal.
8. According to Shakespeare, what is Yorick's profession?
9. Which Scottish island is further north — Benbecula or Barra?
10. What is gerontology the study of — aromatic plants and leaves, sea salts and minerals, the ageing process or ancient European languages?
11. Which name means happiness — Edith, Felicity, Fiona or Hermione?
12. What is the title of the wife of an earl?
13. Name three sayings or proverbs containing a part of your head.
14. Author James Herriot wrote books about his life as what?
15. Name the seventh sign of the Zodiac.
16. Who was born at 17 Brunton Street, London in April 1926?

■ ANSWERS ■

1 Because the skin on your lips is thinner and less oily than other skin, 2 Kenny Dalglish, 3 Harold Wilson. He returned in 1974 after being defeated in 1970. 4 Patricia Routledge, 5 County Down, 6 It's a volcano, 7 The blue whale, 8 Court jester, 9 Benbecula, 10 The ageing process, 11 Felicity, 12 Countess, 13 Walls have ears, Out of the mouths of babes, Don't cut off your nose to spite your face, Take it on the chin etc, 14 A country vet, 15 Libra, 16 Princess Elizabeth, later Queen Elizabeth the Second.

THE SUNDAY POST
FAMILY QUIZ BOOK

SPORT
Play a part!

1. Which nation has been runners-up in football's World Cup the most times?
2. When did Steve Davis win his first World Snooker Championship – 1979, 1981 or 1983?
3. In what sport did Betty Snowball compete for England?
4. What was the score at Old Trafford when Manchester United played Roma in the Champions League in April, 2007?
5. Who replaced Duncan Fletcher as coach of the English cricket team?
6. Which rugby union side are known as the Pumas?
7. In which year did Pakistani cricketer Hanif Mohammad score an innings of 499?
8. Which Portuguese club won the European Cup in 1961 and then again 1962?
9. In which year were the Summer Olympics held in Mexico City?
10. In which sport was Bernie Parent a goalkeeper?
11. From which sport was a Chinese woman called Zhong Weiyue banned for two years?
12. Who was the first British woman to climb Mount Everest?
13. At which super-fast sport was Karl Maier a world champion in the 1980s?
14. Which football team plays at Somerset Park?
15. If you were watching Lokeren play Beveren in a football match, which country would you be in?
16. At which cricket ground did Harold 'Dickie' Bird umpire his last match?

ANSWERS

1 West Germany, 2 1981, 3 Cricket, 4 7-1 to Man United, 5 Peter Moores, 6 Argentina, 7 1958, 8 Benfica, 9 1968, 10 Ice Hockey, 11 Swimming, 12 Rebecca Stevens, 13 Speedway, 14 Ayr United, 15 Belgium, 16 Lord's.

GENERAL KNOWLEDGE

How much do YOU know?

● 1-5 Know a little! ● 6-11 Know a lot! ● 12-16 Know it all!

1. In the song *The Christmas Alphabet* what does 'I' stand for?
2. Is a martingale an African wind, part of a horse's harness or a traditional Maori lullaby?
3. Where was the first Butlin's holiday camp?
4. Why do we put a star at the top of a Christmas tree?
5. Name David Bowie's first hit single.
6. Who is credited with inventing the safety pin — Walter Hunt in 1849, James Starley in 1870 or Gustav Pasch in 1844?
7. Name the sport Harry Potter plays at Hogwarts School.
8. How heavy is the average human brain?
9. If you suffered from chronomentrophobia would you be afraid of clocks, calendars, crows or cheese?
10. If you had a full set of teeth, how many would you have — 20, 26, 32 or 40?
11. Is Prince William right or left-handed?
12. Name the Three Wise Men.
13. Why is the Adam's apple so called?
14. The Anderson air raid shelter took its name from John Anderson MP, who held which cabinet post?
15. In which year did it become compulsory to wear a seatbelt?
16. Where would you find your impedicus — on your bookshelf, in your car or on your hand?

ANSWERS

1 The icing on the cake as sweet as sugar cane, 2 Part of a horse's harness, 3 Skegness, which opened in 1937, 4 It represents the star that led The Three Wise Men to the infant Jesus, 5 Space Oddity in 1969, 6 Walter Hunt in 1849, 7 Quidditch, 8 3lbs/1.4kg, 9 Clocks, 10 32, 11 Left-handed, 12 Gaspar, Melchior and Balthazar, 13 From the idea that a piece of the forbidden fruit stuck in Adam's throat, 14 He was Home Secretary, 15 1983, 16 On your hand. It's your middle finger.

GENERAL KNOWLEDGE

Take the test.

1. Will 2100 be a leap year?
2. In the Rolling Stones' lyric who is a 'gas, gas, gas'?
3. Rearrange THEN GARY SAVED FRUIT to identify a musical.
4. Does blepharitis affect your toenails, kidneys, ears or eyelashes?
5. Where in London does the Ceremony of the Keys take place every night?
6. Does a fright really make your hair stand up?
7. Name three 'golden' birds.
8. Did the UK change over to decimal money in 1971, 1973 or 1975?
9. What colour is the cover of a UK passport?
10. Who bought the Queen her first corgi?
11. Which town in the Scottish borders contains two parts of the face?
12. What are cherubim and seraphim?
13. Name two Bond themes sung by Shirley Bassey.
14. What four-letter word, written in capitals, reads the same forwards, backwards and upside down?
15. Who parachuted into Scotland during 1941 and later was the last resident of Berlin's Spandau Prison?
16. Quasi-autonomous non-governmental organisations are often criticised. How are they more commonly known?

ANSWERS

1 No, 2 Jumping Jack Flash, 3 Saturday Night Fever, 4 Eyelashes, 5 The Tower of London, 6 Yes, Fear causes muscles to contract and hair becomes erect, 7 Golden eagle, golden plover, golden pheasant etc, 8 1971, 9 Burgundy, 10 Her father, King George VI, in 1933, 11 Eyemouth, 12 Angels, 13 Goldfinger, Diamonds Are Forever or Moonraker, 14 NOON, 15 Rudolph Hess, 16 Quangos.

GENERAL KNOWLEDGE

Facts are fun!

1. Which common tree disperses winged seeds that spin through the air?
2. What has a head at one end and a point at the other?
3. Did Donald Duck make his debut in the 1920s, 1930s or 1940s?
4. Where in the UK can you land at North Ronaldsay Airport?
5. Does the band The Stereophonics come from England, Wales, Scotland or Ireland?
6. If a cocktail is made in a 'mist', how is it served?
7. When did we celebrate the 50th anniversary of the Queen's accession?
8. Rearrange I'VE HEARD SID TRIES BED to recall an Evelyn Waugh novel.
9. Which monarch was born on December 7, 1542?
10. The song Danny Boy is set to the music of what?
11. If you sailed in a straight horizontal line from the West Coast of Ireland would you land in Canada or the USA?
12. Mocha is a mixture of which two flavours?
13. If you suffer from ecclesiophobia are you afraid of — criticism, Eccles cakes, churches or handcuffs?
14. *Prepare Ye The Way Of The Lord* is a song featured in which 1970s stage musical?
15. Name the only tune Tom, The Piper's Son could play.
16. If you're enjoying Arbroath smokies, what kind of fish are you eating?

ANSWERS

1 The sycamore, 2 A pin or a nail, 3 1934 in a Disney short called The Wise Little Hen, 4 Orkney, 5 Wales, 6 On crushed ice, 7 2002, 8 Brideshead Revisited, 9 Mary, Queen of Scots, 10 Londonderry Air, 11 Canada, 12 Coffee and chocolate, 13 Churches, 14 Godspell, 15 Over The Hills And Far Away, 16 Haddock.

GENERAL KNOWLEDGE

Quite quizzical!

1. Name *Dr Who's* home planet.
2. Who would wear a mitre?
3. Name an English town which has given its name to a type of carpet.
4. Would it have been possible for someone to climb the Eiffel Tower in Paris in 1870?
5. What was the real name of novelist George Eliot?
6. Which performer always has his back to the audience?
7. Is romano a type of sausage, cheese, bread or wine?
8. 'Tryin' to find lots of things not to do' is a line from which song which featured in a 1949 movie?
9. How many contestants compete in a round of TV's *University Challenge?*
10. What part of the body can be affected by keratitis?
11. Which vegetable can either be a globe or a Jerusalem?
12. What should an avenue have that a street doesn't?
13. Who is your cousin once removed?
14. Name the smallest US state.
15. What fruit is used to make Eve's Pudding — Apricots, bananas, apples or grapefruit?
16. Piob-mhor are something you particularly associate with Scotland. What are they?

ANSWERS

1 Gallifrey, 2 Archbishops and bishops, 3 Wilton or Axminster, 4 No. It was built for the 1889 Paris Universal Exposition, 5 Mary Ann Evans, 6 The conductor of an orchestra, 7 It's a strong tasting hard cheese, 8 Busy Doing Nothing, sung by Bing Crosby in the film A Connecticut Yankee In King Arthur's Court, 9 Eight — two teams of four, 10 It's inflammation of the cornea at the front of the eye, 11 An artichoke, 12 A line of trees, 13 Your cousin's child. The once refers to one generation, 14 Rhode Island, 15 Apples, 16 Bagpipes.

GENERAL KNOWLEDGE

How much do YOU know?

1. What was the second James Bond movie?
2. Could you have watched BBC2 in 1965?
3. 'History will be kind to me for I intend to write it' is a quote from Albert Einstein, Oscar Wilde or Winston Churchill?
4. What is the second line of the hymn *Onward Christian Soldiers?*
5. How should you address a cardinal?
6. What are polders in the Netherlands?
7. North Utsire, South Utsire, Fisher and Humber are all what?
8. How do you write 905 in Roman numerals?
9. What name is given to a charge made by a restaurant for serving wine brought by the customer?
10. Scottish, Manchester and Yorkshire are all types of what?
11. According to Greek mythology, what happened if you looked a Gorgon in the eye?
12. If you ordered stifado in a Greek restaurant what would you expect to receive?
13. If peat is left in the ground for long enough what will it eventually become?
14. Unscramble DULL MIME THEN I'M ONE to reveal a UK landmark.
15. Is a chiminea a wood-burning clay oven, an Indian peace pipe, a mythical bird or a reed pipe wind chime?
16. Name the only country to have reached the finals of every World Cup tournament since the start of the competition in 1930.

ANSWERS

1 From Russia With Love, in 1963, 2 Yes, it began on April 20, 1964, 3 Winston Churchill, 4 Marching as to war, 5 Your Eminence, 6 Areas of low-lying land reclaimed from the sea, 7 Shipping forecast areas in the North Sea, 8 CMV, 9 Corkage, 10 Terrier dog, 11 You turned to stone, 12 A meat dish stewed with onions and sometimes tomatoes, 13 Coal, 14 The Millennium Dome, 15 A wood-burning clay oven, 16 Brazil.

GENERAL KNOWLEDGE

Take the test.

1. Mary, Queen of Scots, was born in which Scottish palace?
2. Is Zara Phillips older than Prince William?
3. In *My Love Is Like A Red, Red Rose* by Burns, he says he'll love thee still my dear — until what?
4. In Greek mythology, which handsome character fell in love with his own reflection?
5. Unscramble A LONE CRAB to reveal a Spanish city.
6. Which soaps do you associate with these cities: a) London, b) Chester, c) Manchester?
7. Why can't a person living in Edinburgh be buried in Glasgow?
8. What's the most common cause of sleeplessness?
9. Do snails have teeth?
10. How should a pianist play a piece of music marked prestissimo?
11. 'I'm going to bounce up and down on my spring' is a line from which well-known Eurovision hit?
12. What is a tarn?
13. Silver Dawn, Camargue and Corniche are all types of what?
14. Which country issues the Krugerrand?
15. Is a lindy hop a tropical lizard, a dance style, an athletics event or a wild flower?
16. What can a bath, a marathon, and a competition all have in common?

══ ANSWERS ══

1 Linlithgow Palace, 2 Yes, by a year, 3 'Till a' the seas gang dry, 4 Narcissus, 5 Barcelona, 6 a) EastEnders, b) Hollyoaks, c) Coronation Street, 7 Because he or she is still alive, 8 Anxiety and stress, 9 Yes. Their tongues are covered in rows of them, 10 Extremely fast, 11 Jack in The Box, sung by Clodagh Rogers in 1971, 12 A small mountain lake, 13 Rolls-Royce car, 14 South Africa, 15 It's a dance done to swing music, 16 You can run them all!

GENERAL KNOWLEDGE

Facts are fun!

● 1-5 Could improve! ● 6-11 Getting better! ● 12-16 The best!

1. In The Bible, how many loaves and fishes did Jesus use to feed the 5000?
2. In which TV soap did Robbie Williams appear as an extra?
3. What animal will not sweat until the temperature reaches 40 degrees Celsius?
4. Which Teletubby carried a handbag?
5. What type of a plant is bamboo?
6. How many 20th Century Prime Ministers did have?
7. Can you think of a figure of speech which ha origins in sprinting?
8. Which city can be found at the northern end of the M1?
9. How did Sir Walter Raleigh meet his gruesome end?

10. When might a small village remind you of a Shakespearean work?
11. What is the world's smallest species of bird?
12. Was Gerald Ford a Democratic or Republican US president?
13. Who might use a piton in their sport?
14. Which country was the first to use number plates on cars?
15. Which spirit is used to make the drink grog?
16. When was the first Isle of Man TT race held — 1907, 1917, 1927 or 1937?

ANSWERS

1 *Five loaves and two fishes.* He appeared in a pub scene, 3 The camel, 4 Tinky Winky, 5 It's a type of grass, 6 20, from the Marquess of Salisbury to Tony Blair, 7 To jump the gun or be quick off the mark, 8 Leeds, 9 He was beheaded in 1618, 10 When the village is a hamlet, 11 The bee hummingbird, 12 Republican, 13 A mountaineer. It's a metal peg or spike driven into rocks for support, 14 France in 1893, 15 Rum, 16 1907.

THE SUNDAY POST FAMILY QUIZ BOOK

GENERAL KNOWLEDGE
Quite quizzical!

● 1-5 Quite quiet! ● 6-11 Quite qualified! ● 12-16 Quite quick!

1. In the JK Rowling novels, how old is Harry Potter when he discovers he's a wizard?
2. The Danube flows through nine European Countries. Can you name five of them?
3. What is a Sam Browne?
4. If a piece of paper measured 210 x 297mm what size would it be — A3, A4, or A5?
5. In what part of your body would you find your mandible — your face, hands or toes?
6. Which country is the most popular tourist destination in the world?
7. Orography is the study of what — mountains, oceans, icebergs or volcanoes?
8. Gentoos, kings, macaronis and rockhoppers are all types of what?
9. Huntingtower Castle can be found outside: a) Dunbar, b) Perth, c) Peebles?
10. Name the second largest island in Mediteranean.
11. Does a pteridologist study fungi, pterodactyls, ferns or fruit flies?
12. Who is the patron saint of fishermen?
13. Did the first bowler hats have anything to do with bowling?
14. According to the saying what do empty vessels make?
15. What was the weather like when Queen Elizabeth II was crowned in Westminster Abbey — dull, bright, showery or snowy?
16. What was the spin-off show to the US soap *Dallas?*

ANSWERS

1 12 years old, 2 Any five from Germany, Austria, Slovakia, Hungary, Croatia, Serbia, Bulgaria, Romania and Ukraine, 3 An over-the-shoulder soldier's belt, 4 A 4, 5 Face. It's your lower jaw bone, 6 France, 7 Mountains, 8 Penguins, 9 Perth, 10 Sardinia, 11 Ferns, 12 St Andrew, 13 No, they were made from felt supplied by Thomas and William Bowler of London, 14 The most noise, 15 Showery, 16 Knots Landing.

GENERAL KNOWLEDGE
How much do YOU know?

● 1-5 Know a little! ● 6-11 Know a lot! ● 12-16 Know it all!

1. Choppers and Chippers were all the rage in the 1970s. What were they?
2. How many characters are in a National Insurance number?
3. Can you think of four boys' names ending in an L?
4. Which canal carries food through the human body?
5. What is somniloquence?
6. Name the colours in the Italian flag.
7. We've all heard of aromatherapy, but what is thalassotherapy?
8. How long is the Channel Tunnel — 21, 31, 41 or 51 miles?
9. We call it a queue, but what is it known as in America?
10. Is a bear paw a style of necktie, sleeve, shoe or hat?
11. When was Alex Salmond first elected as leader of the SNP?
12. Which is the fastest creature on two legs?
13. In *The Selkirk Grace* what comes after, 'Some hae meat and canna eat, and some wad eat that want it'?
14. Why is something that goes too far 'beyond the pale'?
15. Rearrange SHARE ONE PHIL to recall a sixties singing sensation.
16. Was radio invented in the 19th or 20th century?

ANSWERS

1 Bikes with a low front wheel and high handlebars, 2 Nine, 3 Any four from Daniel, Paul, Michael, Neil, Carl, Samuel, Nigel etc, 4 The alimentary canal, 5 Talking in your sleep, 6 Green, white and red, 7 A treatment using sea water and seaweed to promote beauty and nourish health, 8 31 miles, of which 23 are underwater, 9 A line, 10 It's a kind of snowshoe, 11 1990, 12 The ostrich, 13 'But we ha'e meat, and we can eat, Sae let the Lord be thankit,', 14 'Paling is erected to define boundaries, so to be 'beyond the pale' is outside defined boundaries, 15 Helen Shapiro, 16 19th Century. It was patented in 1896.

GENERAL KNOWLEDGE

Take the test.

1. Which royal brother weighed more when he was born — Prince William or Prince Harry?
2. What do the seven spikes on the crown of the Statue of Liberty symbolise?
3. How did Roman Emperor Nero die?
4. The Taj Mahal was built in whose memory?
5. How high is the Millennium Eye — 250ft, 450ft or 700ft?
6. If you suffered from gamophobia what would you be afraid of — music, punishment, marriage or poverty?
7. Can you think of three girls' names beginning with Y?
8. What is an isthmus?
9. Which motor company makes the Calibra and Omega models?
10. Is a clumber a climbing implement, a breed of spaniel, a former make of car or a perennial plant?
11. Which disease was once known as consumption?
12. Tennis elbow and housemaid's knee are forms of which inflammatory complaint?
13. Rearrange I'LL BAR MANDY to find an actor who formerly appeared in *Heartbeat*.
14. If you're reading a Fodor's guide, you're probably thinking of doing what?
15. *The Kilmarnock Edition* features the works of which famous Scotsman?
16. Name the French National Anthem.

◼◼◼◼◼ ANSWERS ◼◼◼◼◼

1 Prince William at 7lbs 1.5oz, Prince Harry weighed 6lb 14oz, 2 The light of liberty shining on the seven seas and seven continents, 3 He committed suicide by stabbing himself, 4 Emperor Shah Jahan's wife, who was known as Mumtaz Mahal (hence Taj Mahal), 5 450ft high, 6 Marriage 7 Yasmin, Yvonne, Yootha, Yolanda etc, 8 A narrow neck of land connecting two larger areas of land, 9 Vauxhall, 10 Breed of spaniel, 11 Tuberculosis, 12 Bursitis, 13 Bill Maynard, 14 Travelling. They're a series of travel guides, 15 It's an edition of the poetry of Robert Burns, 16 La Marseillaise.

GENERAL KNOWLEDGE

Facts are fun!

1. What name did American children give to the toy Action Man?
2. Which country is divided into Cantons?
3. According to legend, which coastal beauty spot in Northern Ireland was created by the giant Finn McCool?
4. What is the Little Minch in Scotland?
5. On which side of the road do they drive in Turkey?
6. Jefferson is the middle name of which British politician?
7. The quote 'an army marches on its stomach' is often attributed to whom?
8. We all carry the products of Llantrisant, near Pontypridd, Wales. What are they?
9. How many ribs do we have?
10. How is the letter O represented in Morse Code — dot dot dash, three dashes or three dots?
11. Can you think of three girls' names ending with the letter H?
12. Identify these British racecourses: a) Scarlet transport, b) washing tub, c) fine pine.
13. What does an ungulate animal have?
14. Does the *Oberammergau Passion Play* in Germany take place every five, 10 or 15 years?
15. A sapphire wedding anniversary is how many years of marriage?
16. Can you think of a Shakespeare play with an English town in its title?

ANSWERS

1 G.I. Joe, 2 Switzerland, 3 The Giant's Causeway. Legend says he fell in love with a lady giant on Staffa and built it to bring her back to Ulster, 4 A stretch of water separating Skye and the Outer Hebrides, 5 The right, 6 William Hague, 7 Napoleon Bonaparte, 8 Coins. It's the home of the Royal Mint, 9 24, 10 Three dashes, 11 Deborah, Hannah, Sarah, Eilidh, Elizabeth etc, 12 a) Redcar, b) Bath, c) Goodwood, 13 Hooves, 14 Every 10 years, 15 45 years, 16 The Merry Wives of Windsor.

The SUNDAY POST FAMILY QUIZ BOOK

GENERAL KNOWLEDGE
Quite quizzical!

● 1-5 Quite quiet! ● 6-11 Quite qualified! ● 12-16 Quite quick!

1. The TV show *Big Brother* always hits the headlines, but in which novel did Big Brother first appear?
2. How old was Alexander Graham Bell when he invented the telephone?
3. If you suffered from stasiphobia what would you be afraid of?
4. Marks & Spencer began in 1884 when Michael Marks hired a stall in which city?
5. The number one with a hundred zeros after it is called a — googol, troogle, diddle or schmoogle?
6. What can you have on both your computer desktop and the walls of your home?
7. Is the postcode for Downing Street, London W1A, WE1, SE1 or SW1A?
8. If the back of a coin is the reverse, what do you call the front?
9. Unscramble DJ LANCE SANG OK to find an actress who turned to politics.
10. 'At first I was afraid, I was petrified' begins which well-known pop song?
11. Can you think of six Scottish towns containing boys' names?
12. What name is given to the lowest price a seller will accept at an auction?
13. In which English city can you visit the Grand Opera House and the Jorvik Centre?
14. In which decade did farthings cease to be legal tender?
15. Where is your popliteal fossa — inside your ear, behind your knee or at the side of your head?
16. Samuel Taylor Coleridge, Robert Southey and William Wordsworth are collectively known as what?

ANSWERS

1 *1984*, by George Orwell, 2 He was 28 when he conducted successful experiments in 1875, 3 Standing upright, 4 Leeds, 5 A googol, 6 Wallpaper, 7 SW1A, 8 The obverse, 9 Glenda Jackson, 10 I Will Survive, sung by Gloria Gaynor, 11 Coupar Angus, Dalkeith, Portpatrick, St Andrews, Johnstone, Peterhead etc, 12 The reserve, 13 York, 14 1960s. It was withdrawn on Dec 31, 1960, 15 Behind your knee, 16 The Lake Poets.

GENERAL KNOWLEDGE

How much do YOU know?

1. How did DIY store B&Q get its name?
2. Is Jersey part of the United Kingdom?
3. Third molars are more commonly known as what?
4. Did Ronald Reagan become president in the late 1970s or early 1980s?
5. Why do we say 'keep your shirt on' to someone losing their temper?
6. Sir Paul McCartney, John McEnroe and Bill Clinton share which physical characteristic?
7. In The Bible, what variety of trees grew in the Garden of Gethsemane?
8. Why is it called a deathwatch beetle?
9. In Terence Rattigan's *The Winslow Boy,* what is Ronnie accused of stealing?
10. Is a viscacha an Italian fruit bush, a Spanish country dance or a South American rodent?
11. With what German liqueur is Black Forest cherry cake usually flavoured?
12. In bygone days, what was a 'penny dreadful'?
13. Mahon is the main city of which Mediterranean island?
14. Give the name of a traditional gent's haircut using four words.
15. Vexillology is the study of timepieces, coats-of-arms, flags or ancient languages?
16. In which Scandinavian country could you visit the cities of Espoo and Turku?

ANSWERS

1 It was founded by Richard Block and David Quayle in Southampton in March 1969. 2 No, but it is a British Crown Dependency, 3 Wisdom teeth, 4 1980s. He was in office from 1981-1989, 5 When shirts were much more difficult and expensive to make, men took them off to avoid damaging them in a fight, 6 They're all left-handed, 7 Olive trees, 8 People once believed the ticking sound it makes forecast a death, 9 A five shilling postal order, 10 A South American rodent, 11 Kirsch, 12 A cheap, sensational story or comic book, 13 Minorca, 14 Short back and sides, 15 Flags, 16 Finland.

ENTERTAINMENT

Are you a star solver?

1. Chewbacca appears in which series of films?
2. Rearrange GEE COOL REG to recall a well-known British TV and movie actor.
3. What's the difference between a symphony orchestra and a philharmonic orchestra?
4. Christopher Davison found fame after changing his name to — Sting, Elvis Costello, Chris de Burgh or Adam Ant?
5. Who wrote the scripts for the BBC sitcom *Dinnerladies?*
6. In music how many quavers make a minim?
7. Who played Marshall P Knutt in *Carry On Cowboy?*
8. Pick the odd one out — *Teletubbies, Sesame Street, Tweenies* or *Rosie And Jim?*
9. Who portrayed the Australian outlaw *Ned Kelly* in the 1970 movie of that name?
10. Magical Mr Mistoffelees is a character in which Andrew Lloyd Webber musical?
11. In which film does the leading man say, 'Do I feel lucky? Well, do ya, punk?'?
12. In which year did the televising of the House of Commons begin — 1985, 1987, 1989 or 1991?
13. Which character was portrayed by Richard Burton in the movie *Cleopatra?*
14. 'Father had a business, strictly second-hand, everything from toothpicks, to a baby grand' are the opening lyrics of which Barbra Streisand song?
15. How many extras did Richard Attenborough hire for the funeral scene of *Gandhi* — 150,000, 300,000, 450,000?
16. Which actress was in both *Men Behaving Badly* and *Where The Heart Is?*

ANSWERS

GENERAL KNOWLEDGE

Take the test.

● 1-5 Must try harder! ● 6-11 Could do better! ● 12-16 Top of the class!

1. Did Sean Connery make more Bond movies than Roger Moore?
2. Name the world's smallest state.
3. Which grow faster — fingernails or toenails?
4. Why are ships' portholes round?
5. How did the foxglove get its name?
6. What was the name of the Queen's first corgi?
7. The first football World Cup took place in 1930 in Uruguay. Where was the second competition held?
8. Which sitcom did Baroness Thatcher once say was her favourite — *Last Of The Summer Wine, Yes, Minister* or *The Good Life?*
9. What is the geographical significance of The Mull of Galloway?
10. What kind of drink is lapsang souchong?
11. If an American describes something as duck soup, what does he mean?
12. To a medic, compound and greenstick are types of what?
13. Vol-au-vents are a popular party snack, but what does it mean in English?
14. Which of the following is not a line on the London Underground — Southern, District, Bakerloo, Northern?
15. Unscramble THE MOUSE RUINS to locate the name of a Scottish Football League club.
16. In the story of *Mary Poppins,* how much does it cost to feed the birds?

ANSWERS

1 No. Both have played Bond in seven films, 2 The Vatican City, 3 Fingernails, 4 They're much stronger than square or rectangular windows, 5 Fox is a corruption of folks, and an old belief stated that the fairy folks sheltered in the flowers, 6 Dookie, 7 Italy in 1934, 8 Yes, Minister, 9 It's Scotland's most southerly mainland point, 10 It's a unique blend of tea from China, 11 It's an easy task, 12 Bone fractures, 13 Flight on the wind, 14 Southern, 15 Stenhousemuir, 16 Tuppence a bag.

GENERAL KNOWLEDGE

Facts are fun!

1. How many bones are there in the human face — 4, 14, 24 or 34?
2. What was John Lennon's middle name?
3. Boris Spassky was famous in which sport?
4. Which member of the Royal Family's names include Elizabeth Alice Louise?
5. Which boy's name appears in most nursery rhymes?
6. According to the proverb, what can't you do if you don't speculate?
7. Which is the longest book in The Bible — Joshua, Proverbs, Leviticus or Psalms?
8. Where did the catchphrase 'Are you sitting comfortably' originate?
9. How many bathrooms are in Buckingham Palace — 28, 48, 78, 108?
10. Ceilidh is the Gaelic word for what — dance, dream, visit or entertainment?
11. In *Star Trek* what is Captain James T Kirk's middle name?
12. Which 1960s singer named his daughter Tulip after the song that made him famous?
13. Solve the following clues to flowers: a) vulpine attire, b) partygoer without partner, c) Remembrance Day flower, d) fragrant Prince.
14. Which district was designated as Britain's first National Park?
15. What is the 49th state of America?
16. What is the Ideo locator on an outdoor map?

ANSWERS

1 14, 2 Winston, 3 Chess, 4 The Princess Royal, 5 Jack, 6 Accumulate, 7 Psalms, 8 In the radio programme, Listen With Mother, 9 78, 10 Visit, 11 Tiberius, 12 Tiny Tim. The song was Tiptoe Thru The Tulips, 13 a) Foxglove, b) wallflower, c) poppy, d) sweet william, 14 The Peak District in 1951, 15 Alaska, admitted in 1959, 16 The 'you are here' arrow.

The SUNDAY POST FAMILY QUIZ BOOK

ENTERTAINMENT

Test your celebrity rating.

● 1-5 Switched off! ● 6-11 Switched on! ● 12-16 Star quality!

1. In the film *Alien,* from which actor's body did the Alien appear?
2. The American comedy series *Frasier* is a spin-off from which other long-running series?
3. What is a nonet?
4. Who starred alongside Mel Gibson in the *Lethal Weapon* series of films?
5. What is unusual about the Dickens novel, *The Mystery of Edwin Drood?*
6. *Pass The Dutchie* was a No.1 hit for which band, back in September 1982?
7. In the TV sci-fi series, *Star Trek: Voyager,* who is captain of the starship?
8. *Little House On The Prairie* and *Bonanza.* Which actor is the connection?
9. William Blake's poem *The Tyger* begins 'Tyger! Tyger! burning bright'. What is the next line?
10. What colour is Superman's cape — red, blue or yellow?
11. Who was in the charts in 1972 with the song *You're So Vain?*
12. Yul Brynner played the Pharaoh and Charlton Heston played Moses in which film?
13. Which fictional character lived at Scatterbrook Farm?
14. *Sticky Fingers* was the title of an album by which perennial band in 1971?
15. Who created the popular children's character, Paddington Bear?
16. 'The truth is out there!' is a quote from which classic TV series?

ANSWERS

BRAINBOX

For smarties only!

1. What is half of a quarter of a third of 48?
2. Is the pylorus in your neck, stomach or shoulder?
3. What are dendrophobic people afraid of?
4. Which is more common in the atmosphere — oxygen or nitrogen?
5. Is jacaranda a tropical tree, a colourful parrot or a strong Mediterranean current?
6. Which scientist wrote the best-selling book, *A Brief History Of Time?*
7. Looking at a rainbow, which colour is on the outside of the curve?
8. Light bulb filaments are made of steel, tungsten or magnesium?
9. Which is the only movable bone in your head?
10. Which term is used to describe the thickness of a liquid?
11. Is osmosis water absorption by plants, shedding of leaves, or the growing of new buds?
12. The four main blood groups are O, A, B and what?
13. Is an analgesic a sleeping pill or a pain reliever?
14. Which kind of lens is thinner in the centre than its edges — concave or convex?
15. Where on your body would you fit puttees — your shoulders, thighs or ankles?
16. The boiling point of water is 100° Centigrade. What is it in Fahrenheit?

ANSWERS

1 Two, 2 Stomach — it's the muscle round the exit from your stomach to the duodenum, 3 Trees, 4 Nitrogen, 5 A tropical tree, 6 Stephen Hawking, 7 Red, 8 Tungsten, 9 The lower jawbone, 10 Viscosity, 11 Water absorption by plants, 12 AB, 13 A pain reliever, 14 Concave, 15 Your ankles, 16 212 degrees Fahrenheit.

GENERAL KNOWLEDGE
Quite quizzical!

1. Britain's first stretch of motorway was opened in December 1958. Did it by-pass — Coventry, Newcastle or Preston?
2. Which TV series was set round a house Queen Victoria almost bought instead of Balmoral?
3. Who is older — Lulu or Cilla Black?
4. Name three animals or birds that have given their names to international rugby teams.
5. Is Westminster's Big Ben the bell or the tower?
6. Name the character played by Johnny Depp in the *Pirates of the Caribbean* movies.
7. Which Welsh sea inlet is something to wear?
8. What do Daniela Bianchi, Molly Peters, Catherina von Schell and Kim Basinger have in common?
9. During the Depression in 1931, an unemployed New York architect called Alfred Butts invented a popular board game. Which one?
10. Which top English football club has a field gun on its badge?
11. Seen on a knitting pattern, what does PSSO indicate?
12. A legendary character in the Wild West had the forenames James Butler. Who was he?
13. What's your star sign if your birthday is on Boxing Day?
14. Is it essential for bride and groom to exchange rings to make a marriage ceremony legal?
15. Name four well-known films whose titles contain a month of the year.
16. What is the capital city of Australia?

ANSWERS

1 Preston (the M6), 2 Monarch of the Glen, which featured Ardverikie House, 3 Cilla was born in 1943, Lulu in 1948, 4 Wallabies (Australia), Springboks (South Africa), Pumas (Argentina), Kiwis (New Zealand) etc, 5 The bell, 6 Captain Jack Sparrow, 7 Cardigan Bay, 8 They all appeared in James Bond films, 9 Scrabble, 10 Arsenal, 11 Pass slipped stitch over, 12 Wild Bill Hickok, 13 Capricorn, 14 No, they're purely symbolic, 15 The Hunt For Red October, Born On The Fourth Of July, April In Paris, Teahouse Of The August Moon etc, 16 Canberra.

GENERAL KNOWLEDGE
How much do YOU know?

1. How did Prestonpans in East Lothian come by its name?
2. In which two modern Scottish counties can you find a River Dee?
3. In the film *Casablanca* what comes after 'Of all the gin joints in all the towns in all the world'?
4. What is the 'luge' in the Winter Olympics?
5. If a medicine is described as a linctus, what does that tell you?
6. Which part of your head might remind you of a church?
7. Rearrange THEN I GET HOT to recall a well-known Elvis Presley recording.
8. How did the expression 'clean as a whistle' originate?
9. Is osnaburg something you would find in a car plant, a farm or a cotton mill?
10. Paul McCartney recorded a version of which well-known nursery rhyme?
11. Grand mal and petit mal are forms of which medical disorder?
12. In rugby, what is the alternative name for the stand-off half?
13. How many spots are there on the three highest dominoes?
14. Which animal is a national symbol of Canada?
15. Do our eyebrows serve any purpose?
16. The Australian recipe 'colonial goose' contains which meat?

ANSWERS

1 It was founded by monks from Newbattle Abbey, hence 'priests' town'. The 'pans' was from the nearby salt pans, 2 Aberdeenshire and Dumfries & Galloway, 3 She walks into mine, 4 Sled racing where competitors lie on their backs and travel feet first, 5 The medicine has been mixed with something sweet to improve the taste, 6 Your temples, 7 In The Ghetto, 8 From when whistle makers had to ensure there was no dirt inside to dampen the tone, 9 A cotton mill, it's a coarse cotton, 10 Mary Had A Little Lamb, 11 Epilepsy, 12 Fly-half, 13 33, 14 Beaver, 15 Yes, they divert sweat from our eyes, 16 Lamb or mutton.

SPORT
Actively awesome!

● 1-5 Relegation! ● 6-11 Mid-table! ● 12-16 Champions!

1. In snooker, which ball has the greater value — brown, yellow or green?
2. If you are a spelunker, does your hobby concern — underground caves, cigarette cards or stamp-collecting?
3. In golf, if a ball is 'pulled' does it finish on the right or the left of the fairway?
4. Are there 11, 13, or 15 players in a Rugby Union team?
5. What is the average weight of a cricket ball?
6. Name the winner of the British Open at Carnoustie in 1999.
7. Eyal Berkovic played for which Scottish football team?
8. Which sport combines cross-country running and map-reading?
9. To the nearest kilometre, how long is a Marathon race?
10. What is the height of the cross-bar of an American Football goalpost? Eight, nine or ten feet?
11. Which horse did Lester Piggot ride to victory in the 1983 Derby? Teenoso or Lucky Lad?
12. Are the Chicago Black Hawks an ice hockey, American football or baseball team?
13. What is the penalty for knocking down a fence in show-jumping?
14. If you had a Cat's Whisker, a Damsel, and a Humungous what might you be interested in?
15. During the 1950s, which sport was dominated by Alberto Ascari and Juan Manuel Fangio?
16. How many times since football's World Cup began has the host nation won?

ANSWERS

ENTERTAINMENT

Are you a star solver?

1. In *Alice's Adventures In Wonderland*, who were at the table with the Mad Hatter?
2. In what year did the Rubik Cube puzzle first go on sale?
3. Which father and daughter sang *Somethin' Stupid* in 1967?
4. Name the actress who played the part of Scarlett O'Hara in the film *Gone With The Wind*?
5. Uriah Heep appears in which Dickens novel?
6. Charles Darrow invented what game in 1931?
7. When Charlotte Church was twelve years old, she had a hit single — what was its title?
8. Who played the only live actor in *Who Framed Roger Rabbit*?
9. Who has a daughter called Sage Moonblood?
10. How many notes are there in an octave — seven, eight or nine?
11. Name the famous novel whose main characters are Piggy, Ralph and Jack.
12. Which part did Larry Hagman play in the US oil barons setting of *Dallas* on TV?
13. Which film star was known as Doris Von Kappelhoff before she became famous?
14. Which town hired the services of the Pied Piper?
15. Who played *The Six Million Dollar Man* and *The Fall Guy*?
16. The Golden Palm is awarded to what or to whom?

ANSWERS

1 The March Hare and the Dormouse, 2 1975, 3 Frank and Nancy Sinatra, 4 Vivien Leigh, 5 David Copperfield, 6 Monopoly, 7 Pie Jesu, 8 Bob Hoskins, 9 Sylvester Stallone, 10 Eight, 11 Lord Of The Flies, by William Golding, 12 JR Ewing, 13 Doris Day, 14 Hamlyn, 15 Lee Majors, 16 The Best Film at Cannes Film Festival.

SPORT
Fit and healthy!

● 1-5 Bronzed off! ● 6-11 Silver lining! ● 12-16 Gold medal!

1. Which horse won the 1980 Grand National — Snowdon or Ben Nevis?
2. Name the five events of the modern pentathlon.
3. Which sport uses the biggest ball?
4. Which British boxer beat Eleoncio Mercedes in 1983 to win the World Flyweight title?
5. Station Park is the home ground of which football team?
6. Who won the Women's Singles at Wimbledon in 1988 — Navratilova or Graf?
7. Which sport is associated with Hurlingham?
8. In what sport do you find a grid-iron?
9. How long is an official game of netball?
10. How many balls are there on a snooker table at the beginning of a frame?
11. Is the Davis Cup awarded for golf, badminton or tennis?
12. In archery, what colour is the centre of the target?
13. Which sporting event starts at Putney and finishes at Mortlake?
14. Name the hard rubber disc used in ice-hockey.
15. Can you name the boxer who was nicknamed the Clones Cyclone?
16. What colours do South African rugby internationalists wear?

ANSWERS

1 Ben Nevis, 2 Fencing, shooting, riding, swimming and running, 3 Basketball, 4 Charlie Magri, 5 Forfar Athletic, 6 Graf, 7 Polo, 8 American Football, 9 Four fifteen-minute quarters making one hour, 10 Twenty-two, 11 Tennis, 12 Gold, 13 University Boat Race, 14 Puck, 15 Barry McGuigan, 16 Green and gold.

GENERAL KNOWLEDGE

Quite quizzical!

1. A golden face mask is given out to winners at which prestigious awards ceremony?
2. The following clues are for words beginning with 'gal': a) swimming tournament, b) brave and heroic, c) Israeli sea.
3. In the Mr Men books, which character has very long arms?
4. What's unusual about the upper set of a goat's teeth?
5. Which planet doesn't have rings — Saturn, Jupiter, Uranus, Mercury or Neptune?
6. How did the expression 'not worth the candle' originate?
7. When would you be most likely to come across a triangulation pillar?
8. Make a connection between Camp David and Shangri-La.
9. Which television personality sailed a boat called Calypso?
10. What is the Triskeles on the Isle of Man?
11. What's so laughable about a famous waterfall in Minneapolis?
12. Which Scotsman became the WBA lightweight boxing champion of the world in 1970?
13. Why do you sometimes see bubbles rising from the bottom of still ponds?
14. Name the second largest city in the USA.
15. We speak about the generation gap, but how many years are in a generation?
16. What's the main difference between peewits and lapwings?

ANSWERS

1 BAFTA Awards, 2 a) Gala, b) gallant, c) Galilee, 3 Mr Tickle, 4 Their two front teeth are missing, 5 Mercury, 6 When candles were expensive, something trivial was said to be not worth burning a candle for, 7 When you're out hillwalking. They're Ordnance Survey obelisks, 8 Shangri-La was the former name of the American presidential retreat, 9 Jacques Cousteau, 10 The three-legged emblem, 11 It's called the Minnehaha Falls, 12 Ken Buchanan, who defeated Ismael Laguna to take the title, 13 Decomposing vegetation creates methane gas, 14 Los Angeles, 15 Around 25-30 years, 16 There's no difference. Peewit is an old country name for a lapwing.

GENERAL KNOWLEDGE

Take the test.

● 1-5 Must try harder! ● 6-11 Could do better! ● 12-16 Top of the class!

1. In the Edward Lear poem, what did the owl and the pussycat take to sea?
2. What does HP in HP sauce stand for?
3. How did plus-four trousers get their name?
4. Is romaine a variety of potato, tomato, carrot or lettuce?
5. Joe, Paul, Mark and Stephen are famous brothers in the acting profession. What is their surname?
6. A Dundee shuffle is something that should be familiar to a ballroom dancer, a bookmaker or a backgammon player?
7. Which two colours designate opposition corners in a boxing ring?
8. Unscramble TEACH A MAN A PLAN to locate a well-known water route.
9. What type of creature is a hairstreak?
10. Which playing card is sometimes called the Black Lady?
11. How many US cents equal a dime?
12. If you 'dosey-do' your partner when dancing, what do you do?
13. In *Romeo And Juliet* is Romeo's surname Montgomery, Montpellier or Montague?
14. Where would you be most likely to see an isohyet?
15. What does the acronym BAFTA stand for?
16. Which European airline consists of three consecutive letters of the alphabet?

ANSWERS

1 Some money and plenty of honey wrapped up in a five-pound note, 2 Houses of Parliament, 3 Because four inches were added to knickerbockers to make them, 4 Lettuce, 5 McGann, 6 A bookmaker. It's a type of bet, 7 Blue and red, 8 The Panama Canal, 9 A butterfly, 10 The Queen of Spades, 11 Ten, 12 Pass each other back to back, 13 Montague, 14 On a map. It's a line connecting points with equal rainfall over a set period, 15 British Academy of Film and Television Arts, 16 KLM.

GENERAL KNOWLEDGE

Facts are fun!

1. When was the wreck of *The Mary Rose* raised?
2. 'She was more like a beauty queen from a movie scene' is how which famous Michael Jackson song begins?
3. Which city saw the birth of Guy Fawkes and the execution of Dick Turpin?
4. What's unusual about a cheetah's claws?
5. The name of which Scottish clan means 'wry mouthed' — Cameron, Campbell, Wallace or Urquhart?
6. Who was Henry VIII's fourth wife?
7. How was Sioux Chief Tatanka Lyotake better known?
8. What job did David Jason do before he was an actor — plumber, piano salesman, electrician or teacher?
9. In *Ali Baba And The 40 Thieves*, what words are used to open the cave?
10. What is *Genevieve* in the British film of that title?
11. What is measured in togs?
12. Why are hallmarks on silver and gold so called?
13. Which major Scottish city's coat of arms features a bird, a fish, a tree and a bell?
14. How many hours behind Greenwich Mean Time is Montreal?
15. Which sign of the Zodiac contains the most letters?
16. For what reason would a doctor use a spirometer?

ANSWERS

1 October 11, 1982, 2 Billie Jean, 3 York, 4 Unlike other cats they're permanently extended, 5 Campbell, 6 Anne of Cleves, 7 Sitting Bull, 8 Electrician, 9 Open, Sesame!, 10 A classic car, 11 Thermal insulation value of duvets, quilts etc, 12 Wardens responsible for stamping it did so in the Goldsmith's Hall in London, 13 Glasgow's, 14 Five hours, 15 Sagittarius, 16 To measure the air capacity of lungs.

KIDS' STUFF

Young at heart!

● 1-5 Year one! ● 6-11 Year four! ● 12-16 Year seven!

1. Which is known as the Eternal City? Rome or Venice?
2. Name the island that lies just off the south coast of Australia.
3. In which French cathedral did Quasimodo live?
4. Where is Beachy Head?
5. The Artful Dodger and Fagin appear in which novel by Charles Dickens?
6. Why did Jack and Jill go up the hill?
7. In which country is Mount Snowdon?
8. Where does *Oor Wullie* live? Auchenshoogle or Auchentoggle?
9. Persian, Manx and Burmese are breeds of which domestic animal?
10. In which city is the TV series *River City* set?
11. Who played Jack Dawson in the film *Titanic*?
12. Fill in the missing word from this story by Roald Dahl. *James and the Giant ____.*
13. What sort of factory did Willy Wonka own?
14. Which cartoon family was created by Matt Groening?
15. Name the capital of Iceland.
16. What is another name for a Yeti?

ANSWERS

1 Rome, 2 Tasmania, 3 Notre Dame, 4 The south coast of England, near Brighton, 5 Oliver Twist, 6 To fetch a pail of water, 7 Wales, 8 Auchenshoogle, 9 Cats, 10 Glasgow, 11 Leonardo DiCaprio, 12 Peach, 13 Chocolate, 14 The Simpsons, 15 Reykjavik, 16 Abominable Snowman.

ENTERTAINMENT
Mostly music!

1. *Mandy* and *Copacabana* are two of this singer's hit songs. Who is he?
2. Who composed the opera *Porgy and Bess*?
3. Who in an orchestra may play a paradiddle?
4. In which year did Dionne Warwick release the evergreen *Do You Know The Way To San Jose?*
5. He's made hit records with Mick Jagger, Bing Crosby and Lenny Kravitz. Name him.
6. On which instrument would you play a madrigal?
7. Who, in 1956, wrote the anti-war protest song *Where Have All The Flowers Gone?*
8. In the Christmas carol, what additional gift did my true love send to me on the Seventh Day of Christmas?
9. Which comedian released a song titled *Don't Laugh At Me?*
10. Which is larger — viola or cello?
11. Who had Top Ten hits in the 1960s with *Matthew And Son* and *I'm Gonna Get Me A Gun?*
12. From which town does the rock band U2 originate?
13. *The Lonely Goatherd* is a song from which very famous stage and film musical?
14. What was the title of the Beatles' last UK No.1 single?
15. How many girls were in the 1980s all-girl band Bananarama — two, three or four?
16. Which country music singer in America made records at two Californian prisons?

ANSWERS

1 Barry Manilow, 2 George Gershwin, 3 The drummer, 4 1968, 5 David Bowie, 6 None — it's a composition for voices only, 7 American folk singer Pete Seeger, 8 Seven swans a-swimming, 9 Norman Wisdom, in 1954, reaching No. 3 in the Charts, 10 Cello, 11 Cat Stevens, 12 Dublin, 13 The Sound Of Music, 14 The Ballad Of John And Yoko, 15 Three, 16 Johnny Cash.

GENERAL KNOWLEDGE
How much do YOU know?

1. Was Mary, Queen of Scots, more than five years old when she was crowned?
2. Which Japanese martial art means 'the gentle art' in English?
3. What are The Honours of Scotland?
4. Bruxism is a habit often picked up in childhood. Is it biting your nails, grinding your teeth or chewing your hair?
5. What term describes public bills introduced to Parliament by peers or back-bench MPs?
6. How did the expression 'to get off on the wrong foot' originate?
7. What are alliaceous vegetables?
8. According to mythology, who is the Roman god of fire?
9. Identify these Books of the Bible: a) an occupation, b) they built straight roads, c) mass departure.
10. What is the largest planet in our solar system?
11. If you had some brilliantine would you: a) rub it on your hair, b) clean your teeth with it, c) polish your silverware?
12. Why are hydrofoil boats so called?
13. What was the former name of New York's John F Kennedy airport?
14. Name the largest gland in the human body.
15. Unscramble I BRING ON ROAD to reveal a useful household object.
16. What was an orraman on a farm or building site?

ANSWERS

1 No, she was only nine months old, 2 Jujitsu, 3 The Royal Regalia or Crown Jewels, 4 Grinding your teeth, 5 Private Members' Bills, 6 It was considered unlucky to get out of bed by putting your left foot on the floor first, 7 Those belonging to the onion family, 8 Vulcan, 9 a) Job, b) Romans, c) Exodus, 10 Jupiter, 11 a) It's a dressing to make hair shiny, 12 They're lifted out of the water by foils or blades that reduce drag and increase speed, 13 Idlewild Airport, 14 The liver, 15 Ironing board, 16 An odd-job man.

GENERAL KNOWLEDGE

Take the test.

1. The song *Barcelona* became an anthem of the 1992 Olympics. Which two singers recorded it?
2. The following answers use the same word twice: a) 1980s new romantic rock band, b) town in New South Wales, c) tropical disease.
3. Which playing card king doesn't have a moustache?
4. 'You're such a lovely audience, We'd like to take you home with us,' are lines from which well-known Beatles song?
5. Who is the Earl of Wessex?
6. Tottenham Hotspur FC play at White Hart Lane in London, but what is a white hart?
7. What's the difference between a couple and a pair?
8. Is your face the only part of your body that blushes?
9. What are crudites on a restaurant menu?
10. Name the world's most northerly capital city.
11. Which actor played Harry in the Harry Potter films?
12. The best mozzarella cheese is made from the milk of which animal?
13. Which monarch succeeded William IV?
14. Hydrophobia is an alternative name for what deadly disease?
15. What's the most commonly observed superstition in Britain?
16. Are Ozzy Osbourne's real first names Oswald William, Horace Raymond, John Michael or Jason Albert?

ANSWERS

1 Freddie Mercury and Montserrat Caballe, 2 a) Duran Duran, b) Wagga Wagga, c) beri-beri, 3 The King of Hearts, 4 Sgt Pepper's Lonely Hearts Club Band, 5 Prince Edward, 6 An albino stag, 7 A pair is two things that match, while a couple is any two, 8 No, blushing can also show down your neck and upper chest, 9 An appetiser of raw vegetables cut into strips, usually served with a dip, 10 Reykjavik, Iceland, 11 Daniel Radcliffe, 12 Buffalo, 13 Queen Victoria, 14 Rabies, 15 Touching wood, 16 John Michael.

GENERAL KNOWLEDGE

Facts are fun!

1. Name any six cuts of beef.
2. Identify these international vehicle registration marks — D, M, PL.
3. Who or what is Jingling Johnnie?
4. Why might you see people running around with the Greek goddess of Victory on their clothes?
5. In music, how many lines are there in a stave?
6. Name two types of 'worm' which aren't really worms.
7. Can a woman marry her widower's brother?
8. What colour is a polar bear's skin?
9. What is the main ingredient of the Chinese dish foo yong?
10. What is the state capital of Utah?
11. Which native bird has the scientific name pica pica?
12. Name the fifth Harry Potter book.
13. Has Cilla Black had any UK No. 1 chart hits?
14. The following clues are for things you might see in garden centres: a) lamp lights, b) money used in gambling, c) old-fashioned sailing ships.
15. How did dungarees get their name?
16. If you suffer from anosmia do you lack the ability to smell properly, tell lies or smile widely?

ANSWERS

1 Sirloin, silverside, topside, brisket, rump etc, 2 Germany, Malta, Poland, 3 It's a percussion instrument consisting of a pole and a crescent hung with bells, 4 Because her name is Nike, 5 Five, 6 Slow-worms, which are legless lizards, and silkworms, which are caterpillars, 7 No — she's deceased, 8 Black. The fur is translucent and looks white, 9 Egg, 10 Salt Lake City, 11 The magpie, 12 Harry Potter and The Order Of The Phoenix, 13 She had two in 1964. Anyone Who Had a Heart and You're My World, 14 a) Bulbs, b) stakes, c) clippers, 15 From the Hindi word dungri, a calico material, 16 Smell things properly.

GENERAL KNOWLEDGE

Quite quizzical!

1. What is the most northerly station on the famous West Highland railway line?
2. When was the Battle of Culloden? 1745, 1746 or 1747?
3. Cathures is an early name for which Scottish city?
4. Which insurance company has a four-coloured umbrella as its logo?
5. What word means a stretch of water and a noise?
6. Why are they called taxi-cabs?
7. On TV, who narrated *The Wombles*?
8. On which Caribbean island is reggae artist Bob Marley buried?
9. In the rhyme, which day's child is full of woe?
10. In English it means 'mixed bits'. Name this popular Chinese meal.
11. Name the Jewish girl who kept a diary while hiding from the Nazis in Amsterdam during World War Two.
12. Films made by which studio began with a flickering transmitter?
13. Which five letter word can follow easy, high, wheel and arm to make four well-known objects?
14. Judges' wigs are traditionally made of what type of hair?
15. Why was it called the H-bomb?
16. What was the name given to Tchaikovsky's Sixth Symphony?

ANSWERS

1 Mallaig, 2 1746, 3 Glasgow, 4 Legal & General, 5 Sound, 6 Taxi is short for taximeter, the device that calculates the fare 7 Bernard Cribbins, 8 Jamaica, 9 Wednesday's, 10 Chop suey, 11 Anne Frank, 12 RKO Radio Pictures, 13 Chair, 14 Horse-hair, 15 It's short for hydrogen bomb, 16 Pathetique.

GENERAL KNOWLEDGE
How much do YOU know?

● 1-5 Know a little! ● 6-11 Know a lot! ● 12-16 Know it all!

1. The Greeks call them the Parthenon Marbles. What do we know them as?
2. BBC wasn't always the British Broadcasting Corporation. What did it stand for originally?
3. The Wilhelmus is the National Anthem of — The Netherlands, Sweden, Denmark or Norway?
4. Identify these wild birds: a) ladle invoice, b) leisure interest, c) magician's bird.
5. Make a connection between Sidney Poitier and Lulu.
6. In China it's traditional for a bride to wear what colour?
7. Name the parents from TV's *The Waltons*.
8. What's the most northerly place you can drive to on the A9 — Dingwall, Wick, Scrabster or Thurso?
9. Your brain makes up what percentage of your body's weight? One, two or three?
10. What is a Lipizzaner?
11. What is the capital of Estonia?
12. Why do jackets often have a vent at the back?
13. Name the tree in the Garden of Eden which bore the forbidden fruit.
14. Are guinea pigs nocturnal?
15. What's the significance of Lizard Point in England?
16. 'If I should die, think only this of me' is a line penned by which poet?

ANSWERS

1 The Elgin Marbles, 2 British Broadcasting Company, 3 The Netherlands, 4 a) Spoonbill, b) hobby, c) merlin, 5 Both starred in the 1960s film *To Sir With Love*, 6 Red, 7 John and Olivia, 8 Scrabster, 9 About two per cent, 10 A breed of horse usually associated with the Spanish Riding School in Vienna, 11 Tallinn, 12 When riding on horseback was the main form of transport, a vent allowed coat tails to fall on either side of the saddle, 13 The Tree of Knowledge, 14 No, 15 It's the UK's most southerly mainland point, 16 Rupert Brooke in *The Soldier*.

THE SUNDAY POST FAMILY QUIZ BOOK

GENERAL KNOWLEDGE
Take the test.

1. Standing outside The Fair Maid's House are you in Dundee, Glasgow, Edinburgh or Perth?
2. The following clues give answers containing the word moon:
   a) James Bond movie, b) TV show with Bruce Willis, c) Glenn Miller favourite.
3. What's the main difference between opera and operetta?
4. Which member of the Royal Family was born in Corfu?
5. Rearrange HEAR PARTNER CRY to reveal the name of a former BBC commentator.
6. If you kow-tow to someone, what do you do?
7. In literature, who rode a horse called Rosinante?
8. What is the main language spoken in Quebec?
9. For what reason would your GP use a sphygmomanometer?
10. One of the following was a real dinosaur, the others are made-up names. Which is the real one — mamenchisaurus, caractadon or plaederactyl?
11. What is fenugreek?
12. In which card game might you hold a full house?
13. If a bird watcher spots a cushat, what has he seen?
14. According to Norse mythology, Valhalla was home to whom?
15. In Islamic culture, what is a fatwa?
16. What does Fitz at the beginning of a surname mean?

ANSWERS
---

1 Perth, 2 a) Moonraker, b) Moonlighting, c) Moonlight Serenade, 3 Operetta is less formal and includes spoken dialogue, 4 Prince Philip, The Duke of Edinburgh, 5 Harry Carpenter, 6 Kneel and touch your head as a sign of respect, 7 Don Quixote, 8 French, 9 To measure blood pressure, 10 Mamenchisaurus, 11 A spice, often used in curries, 12 Poker, 13 It's Scots for wood pigeon, 14 Slain warriors under the leadership of the god Odin, 15 A death decree imposed on an individual, 16 Son of.

GENERAL KNOWLEDGE

Facts are fun!

1. Which uses more muscles — frowning or smiling?
2. Name Tony and Cherie Blair's four children.
3. Geographically speaking, what is a Graham?
4. How did jeeps get their name?
5. Chiroptera is the scientific name for bats, mice or owls?
6. Where in your body is your cochlea?
7. In Rossini's *The Barber Of Seville*, who is the barber?
8. 'Come closer, come closer and listen,' is the first line of which UK Eurovision song?
9. Zoos, greens and locks all have what in common?
10. Name the only Great Lake completely within the USA.
11. Is copra the inside of a chestnut, coconut, date or rambutan?
12. Name the four members of *The Goon Show*.
13. Would you be most likely to see a clarsach in a kitchen, in a garden, on a farm or at a concert?
14. According to Greek mythology, who was the mother of Eros?
15. What does the word safari mean?
16. On a map of the London Underground is the District Line coloured red, green or blue?

ANSWERS

THE SUNDAY POST
FAMILY
QUIZ BOOK

GENERAL KNOWLEDGE
Quite quizzical!

● 1-5 Quite quiet! ● 6-11 Quite qualified! ● 12-16 Quite quick!

1. What's the world's most widely taken drug?
2. Are live lobsters red?
3. Why does cream increase in volume when you whip it?
4. Why do camels have humps?
5. Which Scottish town has a suburb called California — Falkirk, Haddington or Perth?
6. If you were a Sinophile, which country would you like?
7. Why do we call cheap wine plonk?
8. What are 'in velvet' before they're fully mature?
9. How did the umbrella get its name?
10. If glass is laminated, what's been done to it?
11. Which number between one and fifty, when written as a word, is the only number whose letters run alphabetically?
12. When did white £5 notes cease to be legal tender — 1956, 1958, 1959 or 1961?
13. Grimsetter Airport is the old name for a busy Northern Isles airport. But how is it known today?
14. What or who were the Tamworth Two?
15. If an American spends a nickel and tenders a dollar, how much change will he get?
16. In which Girls' Magazine did *The Four Marys* appear as St Elmo's schoolgirls?

═══ ANSWERS ═══

1 Caffeine from tea, coffee, soft drinks etc, 2 No. Colours vary in the sea, 3 Whipping traps air, increasing bulk, 4 It's a store of fat for when food and water are scarce, 5 Falkirk, 6 China, 7 It's probably a corruption of vin blanc, 8 A deer's antlers, 9 From the Latin umbra, meaning shade, 10 It has sheets of plastic material between layers, 11 Forty, 12 1961, 13 Kirkwall Airport, Orkney, 14 Runaway pigs, 15 95 cents, 16 Bunty.

SPORT

True or false – you say which.

1. Red Rum was a famous greyhound.
2. There are ten hurdles in a men's 110m hurdles race.
3. Paula Radcliffe won bronze in the 2004 Olympic Marathon.
4. Steve Redgrave won three Olympic gold medals for rowing.
5. Cricketer Brian Lara's middle name is Charles.
6. Torville and Dean won Olympic gold in 1986.
7. At one time, Sir Alex Ferguson played football for St Johnstone.
8. Steve Davis won his first World Snooker title in 1981.
9. Norwich City are known as the Budgies.
10. Italy beat France in the final of the 2006 World Cup.
11. Hibs reached the final of both Scottish Football cup tournaments in 2007.
12. Footballer Wayne Rooney began his career with Liverpool.
13. Andrew Flintoff is a cricketing Yorkshireman.
14. Golfer Vijay Singh comes from Fiji.
15. Silver Birch won the 2007 Grand National.
16. England's 1966 World Cup winnning captain was Bobby Charlton.

ANSWERS

1 False, he was a racehorse, 2 True, 3 False, she dropped out, 4 False, he won five between 1984 and 2000, 5 True, 6 False, it was 1984, 7 True, 8 True, 9 False, they are the Canaries, 10 True, 11 False, they were beaten in the semi-finals of the Scottish Cup, 12 False, it was Everton, 13, False, he's from Lancashire, 14 True, 15 True, 16 False, it was Bobby Moore.

SPORT
Play a part!

1. In which city do top tennis stars play at the Roland Garros Stadium?
2. Who won the University Boat Race in 2007?
3. What are the four titles that make up a golfing 'grand slam'?
4. The Oval is the home of which English cricket county?
5. Which racquet sport is played on a court that measures 13.4 meters by 6.1 meters?
6. Which famous football player had several nicknames, including the Black Pearl and the King of Football?
7. Which FA Cup Final was known as the White Horse Final? 1923, 1925 or 1927?
8. How many points did Scotland end up with in the Six Nations Championship of 2007?
9. True or false — Manchester United supremo Sir Alex Ferguson started his managerial career with Aberdeen?
10. Who are known as the Hatters?
11. Who defeated Chris Evert in the 1978 Wimbledon Ladies Singles final?
12. In which race would you find the Col du Tourmalet and the Col du Galibier?
13. What is the height of a cricket stump? 24, 26 or 28 inches?
14. Chris Coleman was sacked as manager of which London Premiership club in April 2007?
15. How many professional century breaks have been made by snooker's Stephen Hendry? Over 600 or over 700?
16. Which Scottish rugby team plays at Goldenacre?

ANSWERS

1 Paris, 2 Cambridge, 3 US Masters, US Open, US PGA and the Open, 4 Surrey, 5 Badminton, 6 Pele, 7 1923 West Ham v Bolton, 8 Two, 9 False. He started with East Stirling, 10 Luton Town, 11 Martina Navratilova, 12 Tour de France, 13 Twenty-eight inches, 14 Fulham, 15 Over 700, 16 Heriot's FP.

The SUNDAY POST
FAMILY
QUIZ BOOK

GENERAL KNOWLEDGE

Quite quizzical!

1. How did the expression 'saved by the bell' originate?
2. What is Tiger Woods' first name — Edward, Eldrick or Elroy?
3. Saint Sebastian is the patron saint of athletes, nurses or undertakers?
4. With which instrument would you associate John Williams?
5. The Italian Chapel at Lambholm can be found on which Scottish island?
6. Ronald Villiers is a character in which popular TV comedy series?
7. What is Atholl Brose?
8. Name three of the four US states which border Mexico.
9. Was Ginger Rogers the real name of Fred Astaire's dancing partner?
10. Which star sign covers the period November Twenty-third to December Twenty-first?
11. If you had the letters FRAM after your name, you'd be a Fellow of where?
12. If a bookmaker gave you two monkeys and a pony, how much money would you have?
13. What is vaudeville in the United States?
14. Who was the last Empress of India?
15. What is the connection between *Moonlight*, *Tempest* and *Waldstein*?
16. In which city would you be if you were on the 'rive gauche'?

ANSWERS

1 In boxing, an exhausted fighter could be 'saved by the bell' at the end of a round, 2 Eldrick, 3 Athletes, 4 Guitar, 5 Orkney, 6 Chewin' The Fat, 7 A drink made from whisky, honey, oatmeal and water, 8 Any three from California, Arizona, New Mexico and Texas, 9 No. She was born Virginia Katherine McMath, 10 Sagittarius, 11 The Royal Academy of Music, 12 £1025. £500 times 2, plus £25, 13 Stage entertainment consisting of song and dance acts, acrobats, magicians and comedy sketches, 14 The late Queen Mother. The title was abolished in 1947, 15 They are names of piano sonatas by Beethoven, 16 Paris.

GENERAL KNOWLEDGE

Take the test.

1. If someone offered you a Sally Lunn, would you wear it, plant it in the garden, dance it or eat it?
2. Sherbet is Australian slang for what — toothpaste, beer, barbecues or iced tea?
3. What are the two main towns on mainland Orkney?
4. Strolling down Madison Avenue, you are in which New York borough?
5. The following are clues to well-known films: a) Scottish city reptile, b) metal flowering shrubs, c) male with a precious firearm.
6. Rearrange SEND ON TEA POTS to recall a classic BBC sitcom.
7. What kind of creature is an onager?
8. If you ordered pamplemousse in a Parisian restaurant what would you receive?
9. Is an arctophile a lover of archery, cold climates, dried flowers or teddy bears?
10. Which island is known as the George Cross Island?
11. Name the Greek hero who slew the Minotaur on Crete.
12. What animals have been adopted as symbols of the American Democrat and Republican parties? Horse and oxen, donkey and elephant or lion and antelope?
13. What nationality was the composer Frederick Delius?
14. A green cross by a shop sign indicates what type of business?
15. Ian Hunter was a vocalist with which Seventies pop group?
16. The International Vehicle Registration letter C represents which country?

ANSWERS

1 You'd eat it. It's a sweet bun, 2 Beer, 3 Kirkwall and Stromness, 4 Manhattan, 5 a) Crocodile Dundee b) Steel Magnolias c) The Man with the Golden Gun, 6 Steptoe and Son, 7 A wild ass, 8 Grapefruit, 9 Teddy bears, 10 Malta, 11 Theseus, 12 The donkey (Democrats) and the elephant (Republicans), 13 English, 14 A pharmacy, 15 Mott the Hoople, 16 Cuba.

ENTERTAINMENT

Are you a star solver?

1. He had a No.1 hit in 1984 with *I Just Called To Say I Love You*. Who is he?
2. *La Traviata* is an opera by Wagner, Verdi or Puccini?
3. Name the author who wrote *Misery, Christine* and *Dolores Claiborne*.
4. The films *Schindler's List* and *Jurassic Park* were released in which year?
5. True or false — Bob Dylan has never had a UK No.1 single hit?
6. In the song *I Belong To Glasgow*, how many drinks do I have on a Saturday?
7. Miss Brahms and Pauline Fowler — what's the connection?
8. Did Channel 4 first broadcast in 1980, 1982 or 1984?
9. What kind of animal was Shere Khan in Kipling's *Jungle Book*?
10. Which comedian sang about *Ernie, The Fastest Milkman In The West*?
11. True or false — Julia Roberts starred in the 1993 film, *The Pelican Brief*?
12. In which film did Elvis Presley play the part of a boxer?
13. Did Frodo appear in *Lord Of The Rings,* or *The Hobbit*?
14. Who got to the No.1 spot with *Can The Can* in 1973?
15. In which TV soap might you find Kevin and Sally Webster?
16. Fill in the missing colours to find a song, a film and a TV programme.
    _____ Haze, Clockwork _____ , ____Dwarf.

ANSWERS

1 *Stevie Wonder*, 2 *Verdi*, 3 *Stephen King*, 4 *1993*, 5 *True — his highest position was No.4*, with *Like A Rolling Stone*, *in 1965*, 6 *A couple*, 7 *Wendy Richard played both characters*, 8 *1982*, 9 *A tiger*, 10 *Benny Hill*, 11 *True*, 12 *Kid Galahad*, 13 *Lord Of The Rings*, 14 *Suzy Quatro*, 15 *Coronation Street*, 16 *Purple Haze, Clockwork Orange, Red Dwarf.*

GENERAL KNOWLEDGE

How much do YOU know?

1. The oldest licensed distillery in the world can be found in: a) the UK, b) Germany, c) Denmark, d) Irish Republic?
2. Name the Queen's bodyguard in Scotland.
3. 'No hell below us above us only sky' is a line from which famous pop song?
4. Which dance, performed to Latin American music, is the Spanish word for sauce?
5. If you're driving a Yaris are you behind the wheel of a Nissan, Honda, Mitsubishi or Toyota?
6. We've all heard of Gilbert and Sullivan's *The Mikado*, but who or what is a Mikado?
7. Why do we say 'mark my words' to stress a point?
8. Yuri Gagarin was the first man in space. Name the craft that took him there.
9. What building stands on the corner of New York's Fifth Avenue and 34th Street?
10. Does a luthier make stringed instruments, arrows, playing cards or handbags?
11. Who created the pilot Biggles?
12. Who had 'the face that launched a thousand ships'?
13. The Hubble telescope is often in the news. What nationality was its inventor?
14. On a map of the London Underground is the Circle Line coloured black, blue or yellow?
15. If you asked a bartender for a Screwdriver what would you get?
16. Do willow trees lose their leaves in winter?

ANSWERS

1 The UK, The Old Bushmills Distillery, Co Antrim, Northern Ireland, which was granted a licence to distil in 1608, 2 The Royal Company of Archers, 3 Imagine by John Lennon, 4 Salsa, 5 Toyota, 6 A former title for the Emperor of Japan, 7 You're inviting the other person to write down what you've said for future reference. 8 Vostok 1, 9 The Empire State Building, 10 Stringed instruments, 11 WE Johns, 12 Helen of Troy, 13 Edwin Hubble was American, 14 Yellow, 15 Vodka and orange juice, 16 Yes, they're deciduous trees.

KIDS' STUFF
Young at heart!

● 1-5 Year one! ● 6-11 Year four! ● 12-16 Year seven!

1. In the nursery rhyme, on what did Little Miss Muffet sit?
2. In which city is John Lennon Airport?
3. Which is larger in area, France or Germany?
4. What is the street in London that was once famous for newspaper publishing?
5. Which is the biggest US state?
6. Who are Donatello, Leonardo, Michelangelo and Raphael in cartoons?
7. In which comic would you find Bananaman?
8. Name the scatty verger in *The Vicar of Dibley*?
9. Where is the Suez Canal?
10. If you were watching Juventus play Inter, which country would you be in?
11. What story by Ian Fleming features an amazing flying car?
12. Which nationality are the group Red Hot Chilli Peppers?
13. Christiano Ronaldo plays for which country?
14. Which name is missing from this Girls Aloud line-up? Cheryl, Nadine, Sarah and Kimberley.
15. In which novel would you find the characters David Balfour and Alan Breck Stuart?
16. True or False — David Jason played the part of Rodney Trotter in *Only Fools and Horses*?

■ **ANSWERS** ■

1 A tuffet, 2 Liverpool, 3 France, 4 Fleet Street, 5 Alaska, 6 Teenage Mutant Hero Turtles, 7 The Dandy, 8 Alice, 9 The Middle East, 10 Italy, 11 Chitty Chitty Bang Bang, 12 American, 13 Portugal, 14 Nicola, 15 Kidnapped, 16 False. He played the part of Derek Trotter.

GENERAL KNOWLEDGE

How much do YOU know?

1. Is a 'wrass' a savoury Mexican wrap, a fish or a slang word for a tell-tale?
2. Which famous toy is manufactured in Geingen, Germany?
3. What is regarded as the death card in a pack of playing cards?
4. Professor Van Helsing was a character in which series of famous films?
5. Do car airbags stay inflated after a crash?
6. Should a player have 12, 16 or 24 pieces at the start of a game of draughts?
7. Complete the quote by Tennyson, 'Tis better to have loved _____'
8. Identify the following John Wayne films: a) Horse-drawn vehicle, b) 1960s pop group, c) real stamina.
9. How many finger holes should you find on a penny whistle — three, four, six or seven?
10. We all know the song *Auld Lang Syne*, but what does the phrase mean?
11. How should steak tartare be cooked?
12. Which member of the Royal Family owns Highgrove House?
13. If someone gave you a carimbo would you keep it in a tank, eat it, beat it or sit in it?
14. Name the city which hosted the 2007 Eurovision Song Contest?
15. Which golf course hosted the 2000 Open Championship?
16. Which king led the English army at the Battle of Bannockburn?

ANSWERS

1, A species of fish, 2 Steiff teddy bears, 3 Ace of Spades, 4 Dracula films, normally played by Peter Cushing, 5 No. They are designed to deflate after they have done their job, 6 12 pieces, 7 And lost than never to have loved at all, 8 a) Stagecoach, b) The Searchers, c) True Grit, 9 Six holes, 10 The olden days, or days gone by, 11 It shouldn't be cooked at all. It's a mixture of raw mince and raw egg, 12 Prince Charles, 13 Beat it. It's a drum of African origin, 14 Helsinki, 15 The Old Course, St Andrews, 16 Edward II.

GENERAL KNOWLEDGE
Take the test.

1. Pick the odd one out — Tony Gubba, John Motson, George Alagiah, Eddie Butler.
2. Solve the following clues to Scottish islands: a) mixed up tube, b) high above us, c) where there's brass, d) tasty with bacon.
3. In the 1960s, what were Caroline, London and Scotland?
4. Name three films with compass points in their titles.
5. What old Ford car is also a light wind?
6. Name the cartoon dogs in: a) *Garfield*, b) *Peanuts*, c) *Wacky Races*.
7. Complete the title of the JK Rowling novel *Harry Potter And The Goblet Of* ___.
8. Who said 'The British are a nation of shopkeepers'?
9. The adjective glossal refers to which part of the body?
10. How many stars are on the Australian flag — four, five, six or seven?
11. If someone gave you a sampan would you sail in it, cook in it, wrap it around your shoulders or hang it on your wall?
12. Fran Healy found fame as the singer in which Scottish band — Del Amitri, Simple Minds, Travis or Marillion?
13. What term describes the weight of a motor car without occupants or baggage?
14. What American city did Marc Cohn, Chuck Berry and Mott the Hoople all sing about?
15. Is it more or less than 25 years since Elvis Presley died?
16. Which river runs through Blairgowrie?

ANSWERS

GENERAL KNOWLEDGE
Quite quizzical!

1. What snappy creature featured in hits for both Elton John and Jimmy Nail?
2. What becomes a silverback at around age 15?
3. Which prestigious car manufacturer produced the Testarossa?
4. Who lives on the Island of Sodor?
5. Robert De Niro and Christopher Walken played Russian roulette in which well-known film?
6. When did the first National Lottery draw take place?
7. What word can come after bull, iron and behind?
8. Complete the proverb, 'Many a mickle _____'
9. What is piri piri on a restaurant menu?
10. The surname Wainwright has its origins in which trade — tapestry weaving, bookbinding, wagon making or pipe making?
11. Is the maximum legal length of a cricket bat more or less than three feet?
12. From the Greek meaning 'a garden of flowers', this word is a collection of an author's or musician's work.
13. *A Life On The Ocean Wave* is the march of which military organisation?
14. If you had a shofar would you blow it, ride on it or collect coins in it?
15. Which well-known award was originally called the Statue of Merit?
16. Fidelity, Bravery, Integrity is the motto of which American organisation?

ANSWERS

1 *Crocodile*, as in *Crocodile Rock* and *Crocodile Shoes*, 2 A male gorilla, when the hair on its back turns silver-grey, 3 *Ferrari*, 4 *Thomas the Tank Engine and friends*, 5 *The Deer Hunter*, 6 *November 19, 1994*, 7 *Bars*, 8 *Makes a muckle*, 9 *A hot sauce made with red peppers*, 10 *Wagon making*, 11 *More. They're 38 inches/96.5cm long*, 12 *Anthology*, 13 *The Royal Marines*, 14 *You'd blow it. It's a ram's horn used as a wind instrument*, 15 *The Oscar*, 16 *The FBI.*

GENERAL KNOWLEDGE

Facts are fun!

1. Who was the first female newsreader on BBC national TV news?
2. Big Brother winner Cameron Stout hails from where?
3. The Swedish flag shows a yellow cross on what colour background?
4. What is the 'Auld Clay Biggin' in Ayrshire?
5. Which famous American jazz singer was known as Sassy or the Divine One?
6. Unscramble TUBE HIT ITALIAN IRON to identify a hospital department.
7. Which district of Edinburgh has the same name as a city in Israel?
8. How many books of The Bible end with the letter 'b'?
9. Is the world's largest art gallery in Paris, London, New York or St Petersburg?
10. Name the most northerly county in Ireland.
11. What are lederhosen, once popular in Germany, Austria and Switzerland?
12. Baobabs can be found in India and Africa — but what are they?
13. How did the archer fish get its name?
14. What's the earliest wedding anniversary for which you can receive a card from the Queen?
15. What is the opposite of explosion?
16. Why do flamingos stand on one leg?

ANSWERS

1 Nan Winton in 1960, 2 Orkney, 3 Blue, 4 The Alloway cottage where Robert Burns was born, 5 Sarah Vaughan, 6 Rehabilitation Unit, 7 Joppa, 8 Just one, the Book of Job, 9 It's the Winter Palace in St Petersburg, 10 Donegal in the Republic of Ireland, 11 Short leather trousers, 12 Types of tree, 13 It fires jets of water at insects above the surface of the water and knocks them down, 14 Diamond anniversary (60 years), 15 Implosion, 16 They're just resting the other leg and keeping it warm.

THE SUNDAY POST
FAMILY
QUIZ BOOK

BRAINBOX

For smarties only!

1. If a surgeon is repairing a cleft palate, which area of the body is he working on?
2. What does a commutator do to electric current?
3. Can a wasp sting more than once?
4. Is herpetology — the study of disease, crocodiles or lace-making?
5. On a road map, what does a white 'i' on a blue square represent?
6. What is the difference between your biceps and your triceps?
7. On a suit of armour, which part of your body would a greave protect?
8. Which number can't be represented in Roman numerals?
9. Would a caliologist study — birds' nests, flags or the sun's rays?
10. From which raw ore do we get uranium?
11. Is hafnium — a metallic element used in nuclear reactors or a mythical half witch/half dog?
12. What is St Elmo's Fire?
13. When was the stethoscope, as we know it today, invented?
14. What is a Kentish Glory?
15. What causes tides in the oceans?
16. Would you find a peduncle on a flower, on someone's foot, or on a musical instrument?

ANSWERS

1 The roof of the mouth, 2 Alters its direction, 3 Yes, 4 Crocodiles, 5 Information — from a Tourist Information Centre, 6 Biceps are the muscles which bend the arms, triceps are the ones which straighten them, 7 The shin, 8 Zero, 9 Birds' nests, 10 Pitchblende, 11 A metallic element used in nuclear reactors, 12 A static electricity discharge, 13 In 1855, by an American doctor, Camman, 14 A butterfly, 15 The gravity pull of the moon, 16 On a flower — it's a stalk.

ENTERTAINMENT

Test your celebrity rating.

1. *Club Tropicana* by Wham got to No.1 in the charts in which year?
2. In which Shakespeare play did Shylock bargain with Antonio for a pound of flesh?
3. Who painted *The Birth of Venus*?
4. Who played the title role in the film *Lawrence Of Arabia*?
5. How many different pieces are there in a game of chess?
6. In what year did the Village People have a hit with *Y.M.C.A.*?
7. In the novel *The Jungle Book* what kind of creature was Rikki-Tikki-Tavi?
8. His films include *Two-Way Stretch*, *Dr. Strangelove* and *I'm All Right, Jack*. Who is he?
9. In music, what is the meaning of the term 'lento'?
10. Is the song *Oh, What A Beautiful Mornin'!* from the musical *Showboat*, *Oklahoma* or *Funny Girl*?
11. Is Lesley Garrett — a Breakfast TV Presenter, an opera singer or a film star?
12. In the film *Gone With the Wind* which southern city was burned to the ground?
13. What is the main object of the card game, Pontoon?
14. *Going Postal*, *Thud!* and *Guards, Guards!* are all books by which author?
15. In which year was the film *Alien* released — 1978, 1979, 1980 or 1981?
16. According to the musical, how often does the Highland village of *Brigadoon* appear?

ANSWERS

1 It didn't happen. The song peaked at No. 4 in 1983, 2 The Merchant Of Venice, 3 Botticelli, 4 Peter O'Toole, 5 Six, 6 1978, 7 A mongoose, 8 Peter Sellers, 9 Slow, 10 Oklahoma, 11 An opera singer, 12 Atlanta, 13 To achieve a score of 21, or as near to it as possible, 14 Terry Pratchett, 15 1979, 16 Once every 100 years, for one day only.

ENTERTAINMENT

Are you a star solver?

1. What was shared by the writers Anne, Emily and Charlotte?
2. Who had a hit with *Halfway To Paradise* in 1961?
3. Henry Fonda won an Oscar in 1981 for which film?
4. Fill in the colours of the Sherlock Holmes stories — *A Study In _____ , The _____ Carbuncle.*
5. The Faces and the Barracudas were the gangs in which well-known film?
6. Who created the furious creature called the Bandersnatch?
7. Who had a hit in January 1988 with the song *Sign Your Name?*
8. In the nursery rhyme, to where would you *Ride a Cock Horse*?
9. Gollum's original name in *Lord of the Rings* was what — Smeagol, Samgee or Smee?
10. Who was the central character in Jules Verne's *Around The World In Eighty Days?*
11. What was the record label founded by the Beatles in the 1960s?
12. Name the novel which was a sequel to *Kidnapped* by RL Stevenson.
13. Was Gustav Mahler a painter, composer or scientist?
14. Name the film actress who starred in *The Blue Angel,* a 1930 film.
15. Who was Scheherezade?
16. *Rubber Bullets, I'm Not In Love* and *Dreadlock Holiday* were three of this band's hits. Who were they?

ANSWERS

1 The surname Bronte, 2 Billy Fury, 3 On Golden Pond, 4 Scarlet, green, 5 Saturday Night Fever, 6 Lewis Carroll, 7 Terence Trent D'Arby, 8 Banbury Cross, 9 Smeagol, 10 Phileas Fogg, 11 Apple, 12 Catriona, 13 Composer, 14 Marlene Dietrich, 15 The Storyteller in the Arabian Nights tales, 16 10 CC.

GENERAL KNOWLEDGE
Quite quizzical!

1. What was Northumberland garden designer Lancelot Brown's nickname?
2. Pick the odd one out — saucepan, balti, wok, sampan.
3. Name the first *Carry On* film.
4. If an animal is edentate it has few, if any, what?
5. The Romans called Scotland Caledonia, but what did they call Ireland?
6. What does a chef mean when he describes his special recipe as being devilled?
7. What's the male equivalent of a Dame?
8. Unscramble I'D NET WARM TRAY to locate a productive hospital department.
9. Which two colours feature on the flag of China?
10. Ethylene glycol is better known to motorists as what?
11. What is the setting for Tony Roper's play *The Steamie?*
12. Who had a private plane called *The Lisa Marie?*
13. Which starsign, sometimes known as the water carrier, comes between a goat and a fish?
14. A browband is something you would fit before doing what?
15. The Americans call it a stroller. What name do we know it by in this country?
16. In 1946 the first television licences were issued. How much were they?

ANSWERS

1 Capability, because he had a habit of saying a place had 'capabilities', 2 Sampan is a Chinese boat, while the others are cooking pots, 3 Carry On Sergeant in 1958, 4 Teeth, 5 Hibernia, 6 It's highly seasoned or coated in condiments, 7 Knight, 8 Maternity ward, 9 Red with yellow stars, 10 Anti-freeze, 11 A Glasgow wash house, 12 Elvis Presley, named after his daughter, 13 Aquarius, 14 Riding a horse. It's a part of the bridle, 15 A pushchair, 16 £2.

THE SUNDAY POST
FAMILY
QUIZ BOOK

GENERAL KNOWLEDGE
It's a festive fizzer.

1. What can be mulled to make a festive drink?
2. Scots actor Andy Gray is a regular on the panto circuit, but in which Scottish town was he raised — Polmont, Perth or Peterhead?
3. Name four of the reindeer from the poem *The Night Before Christmas?*
4. Unscramble I'D TRY ANY COIN I SOLD CAVE to reveal a popular Christmas carol.
5. What was No.1 in the pop charts at Christmas 2005?
6. Which ex-*EastEnders* characters were married on Christmas Day 2003?
7. Widow Twanky appears in which popular Christmas panto?
8. Christmas Island in the Indian Ocean is administered by which country?
9. Feliz Navidad is Merry Christmas in Spanish, Italian, Portuguese or Dutch?
10. Who is believed to have been born in Patara, Turkey?
11. Which of the following celebrities was born on December 25:
    a) Carol Vorderman, b) George Clooney, c) Annie Lennox,
    d) Noel Edmonds?
12. Who is credited with introducing Christmas trees to Great Britain?
13. Perfume is a popular gift at Christmas, but what's the world's best-selling fragrance?
14. Christmas Day wasn't a public holiday in Scotland until nearly the end of which decade?
15. Which well-known author wrote *Letters From Father Christmas?*
16. Advent is the period leading up to Christmas Day. When does it begin?

ANSWERS

1 Wine, 2 Perth, 3 Dasher, Dancer, Prancer, Vixen, Comet, Cupid, Donner, Blitzen, 4 Once In Royal David's City, 5 That's My Goal by Shayne Ward, 6 Alfie Moon and Kat Slater, 7 Aladdin, 8 Australia, 9 Spanish, 10 St Nicholas, 11 Annie Lennox, 12 Prince Albert, husband of Queen Victoria, 13 Chanel No.5, 14 The 1950s (1958), 15 JRR Tolkein, 16 The fourth Sunday before Christmas.

THE SUNDAY POST
FAMILY
QUIZ BOOK

GENERAL KNOWLEDGE

How much do YOU know?

1. Which number was the first ever to be drawn in the National Lottery?
2. People who are stereotyped are 'tarred with the same brush'. Why?
3. Who worship in Kingdom Halls?
4. Why are special 'red letter' days so called?
5. Basing his year of birth on the release of his first official film, has Bugs Bunny celebrated his 65th birthday yet?
6. Whose portrait appeared on the famous Penny Black stamp?
7. Did Sean Connery ever win Mr Universe?
8. Why do we call rich people 'well-heeled'?
9. Identify the following Rogers: a) pirate's flag, b) Bob Hoskins' animated sidekick, c) *Beano* boy.
10. Raphus Cucullatus has been extinct since the 17th Century. What's this creature's common name?
11. What shape is the body of a balalaika musical instrument?
12. What does tincture mean in tincture of iodine?
13. In a restaurant, what type of dish is a blanquette?
14. What colour was the first Coca-Cola?
15. Is a hooktip a fish, moth or bird?
16. Name the Ewing ranch in the US TV soap *Dallas*.

ANSWERS

1 30, 2 Farmers used to treat sores on sheep with tar brushes, so those from the same flock were tarred with the same brush, 3 Jehovah's Witnesses, 4 Saints days and church festivals were printed in red in calendars and prayer books, 5 Yes, He made his debut in the 1940 cartoon A Wild Hare, 6 Queen Victoria, 7 No, but he came third in 1953, 8 Because poor people couldn't afford decent shoes, 9 a) Jolly Roger, b) Roger the Dodger, c) Roger the Rabbit, 10 The dodo, 11 Triangular, 12 It's a small amount of iodine mixed with alcohol, 13 French-style stew cooked in a white sauce, 14 The same colour as it is now, 15 A moth, 16 Southfork.

GENERAL KNOWLEDGE

Quite quizzical!

1. In the saying, what begins with a single step?
2. The following answers contain the word moon: a) A David Niven autobiography, b) Theme from *Breakfast at Tiffany's*, c) A Bond film.
3. If you have gynephobia do you fear noises, women or insects?
4. How many surnames in Scotland begin with Mac or Mc — 1 in 4, 1 in 6, 1 in 8 or 1 in 10?
5. How was Mary of Modena's son best known?
6. Which is the only place name in the UK with an exclamation mark?
7. When was the Easter Rising in Dublin?
8. Why do we call a black profile a silhouette?
9. Are turophiles lovers of cheese, cigars, real ale or brandy?
10. What term describes someone who stops being a friend in difficult times or circumstances?
11. What would a sommelier do for a living — pollinate flowers, serve wine or chauffeur VIPs?
12. The expression 'manna from heaven' means unexpected, but very welcome, help. How did the saying originate?
13. SARS is a viral infection that caused panic in parts of the world. What does it stand for?
14. *I Whistle A Happy Tune* is a song from which popular musical?
15. What can be apple, Lincoln or bottle?
16. Is a ganzey something to wear, play, eat or keep in a farmyard?

ANSWERS

1 *Every journey*, 2 a) *The Moon's* A Balloon, b) *Moon River*, c) *Moonraker*, 3 *Women*, 4 *Around* 1 in 8, 5 *The* Old Pretender, 6 *Westward Ho! on the Devon coast*, 7 *1916*, 8 *From the* French Minister of Finance, Étienne de Silhouette *(1709-1767)*, whose hobby was cutting profiles from black paper, 9 *Cheese*, 10 *A fair-weather friend*, 11 *Serve wine*, 12 *In The Bible*, manna *(a nutritious tree extract) was miraculously supplied to the Israelites in the wilderness*, 13 *Severe Acute Respiratory Syndrome*, 14 *The King And I*, 15 *The colour green*, 16 *Wear. It's an old word for a pullover*.

ENTERTAINMENT
Are you a star solver?

1. Was Bob Dylan born in 1939, 1941 or 1943?
2. Jemima Puddle-Duck is a character created by whom?
3. How is the musical instrument known as a dulcimer played?
4. Who are the stars of the 1993 film *Sleepless In Seattle?*
5. Miss Prism is a character from which famous play?
6. *Apache, Kon-Tiki, Geronimo, Atlantis* — what's the connection?
7. Name the character who was in charge of the kitchen in the classic TV series *Upstairs Downstairs.*
8. Cruella DeVille is the villainess in which children's film?
9. When was Brigitte Bardot born — 1932, 1934 or 1936?
10. 'Cutty' means what, in the term, cutty sark, from the Burns poem?
11. Complete the programme — *Sabrina The Teenage* _____.
12. Hazel, Bigwig, Blackberry and General Woundwart appeared in which book?
13. 'By oppression's woes and pains' is a line from which famous song?
14. Gary Cooper won an Oscar in 1932 for which film?
15. What is the term for poetry which doesn't rhyme?
16. Can you name the island in the children's TV series *Thunderbirds?*

ANSWERS

GENERAL KNOWLEDGE

How much do YOU know?

● 1-5 Know a little! ● 6-11 Know a lot! ● 12-16 Know it all!

1. What makes stainless steel stainless?
2. Name four groups beginning with 'New' who have had British pop chart hits.
3. Is George W Bush the forty-first, forty-second or forty-third US President?
4. What is a VIN check?
5. Dogmatix, Getafix and Vitalstatistix are characters in which cartoon series?
6. Gozo and Comino are neighbouring islands of which popular holiday destination?
7. What is jambalaya?
8. Which is older — a veteran car or a vintage car?
9. Who are the RMP in the Services?
10. Name the famous bell at Lloyd's of London.
11. Pick the odd one out — Dunkeld, Jedburgh, Kinross, Melrose.
12. What five letter word can come before biscuit and fall and after spring?
13. What, in France, is a 'trottoir'?
14. Who composed the *Brandenburg Concertos?*
15. Which was the last battle to have been fought on British soil?
16. CV Stanford was: a) a writer, b) a composer or c) an artist?

ANSWERS

1 It is alloyed with elements including chromium that prevent rust, 2 Any five from New Seekers, New Kids On The Block, New Order, New Musik, New Model Army, New World etc, 3 Forty-third, 4 A vehicle identification number check on a car, 5 Asterix the Gaul, 6 Malta, 7 A spicy Creole dish of rice and vegetables, cooked with meat, 8 A veteran car, which is a vehicle which dates from before 1919. Vintage cars date from 1919-1930, 9 The Royal Military Police, 10 The Lutine Bell, 11 Kinross. The other three have an abbey, 12 Water, 13 A pavement, 14 JS Bach, 15 Culloden, 16 A composer.

GENERAL KNOWLEDGE

Take the test.

1. Visiting the CN Tower are you on holiday in Toronto, London, Sydney or Auckland?
2. Raynaud's Disease usually affects what part of the body?
3. WAP phones allow you to access information from the Internet. What does WAP stand for?
4. How many counties in the Republic of Ireland border Northern Ireland?
5. Why is foolscap paper so called?
6. Which UK No.1 hit included the line, 'Each had a wooden horse'?
7. Name the twins who make up the singing group The Proclaimers.
8. Which Scots song contains the line 'O ye'll tak' the high road'?
9. How many operas did Beethoven write?
10. In the USA, what is a freshman?
11. Unscramble HUSH ALL THREE to locate an Edinburgh music venue.
12. How did the drink Bourbon come by its name?
13. In which year did the first Comic Relief appeal take place?
14. Would you find a nosegay in an aviary, in a flower shop or in a bakery?
15. Who was 'The Young Pretender'?
16. Which is the most northerly of the Great Lakes?

ANSWERS

1 Toronto, 2 Hands and fingers. They appear cold due to narrowing of blood vessels, 3 Wireless Application Protocol, 4 Five — Donegal, Cavan, Monaghan, Leitrim and Louth, 5 It originally bore a picture of a fool in a cap in the watermark, 6 Two Little Boys, by Rolf Harris, 7 Craig and Charlie Reid, 8 Loch Lomond, 9 One. Fidelio, 10 A first year college or university student, 11 The Usher Hall, 12 It was first produced in Bourbon County, Kentucky, 13 1985, 14 Flower shop — it's a small bouquet, 15 Bonnie Prince Charlie, 16 Lake Superior.

GENERAL KNOWLEDGE

Facts are fun!

1. What word can describe a dog's ailment and a type of paint?
2. Faroukh Bulsara found fame as a pop star after he changed his name to what?
3. Robusta, Arabica and Liberica are thoroughbred racehorses, coffee beans or fishing rods?
4. Fred Quimby's name was often seen on TV in the credits at the end of: a) *Coronation Street,* b) *Felix The Cat* or c) *Tom And Jerry*?
5. How does pilsner beer get its name?
6. Is logophobia a fear of words, trees or darkness?
7. Yell, Unst and Hoy are all islands. But which of the three is the odd one out?
8. What is a gaucho in South America?
9. Who were Anne Bonny and Mary Read?
10. In which year was the Battle of Waterloo?
11. Under which name did Helen Porter Mitchell achieve fame in the opera world?
12. What year is represented by MCMXCVII in Roman numerals?
13. 'To be, or not to be' is a line from which Shakespeare play?
14. What is a tocsin? A bell, a poison or a song?
15. Name Violet Elizabeth Bott's male sidekick.
16. Why is the dish made up of fried cabbage and potatoes called bubble and squeak?

ANSWERS

1 Distemper, 2 Freddie Mercury, 3 Coffee beans, 4 Tom and Jerry. He directed the famous cartoons, 5 It was first brewed in Plzen (Pilsen), Czech Republic, 6 Words, 7 Hoy, which is in the Orkneys. The other two are Shetland islands, 8 A horseman and cowhand, 9 The only two known women pirates, 10 1815, 11 Dame Nellie Melba, 12 1997, 13 Hamlet, 14 An alarm bell, 15 Just William, 16 From the noise it makes in the pan during cooking.

GENERAL KNOWLEDGE
How much do YOU know?

● 1-5 Know a little! ● 6-11 Know a lot! ● 12-16 Know it all!

1. What kind of fruit is a pomello?
2. A Ruby Wedding is celebrated after how many years?
3. Can you name at least three of the Presidents depicted on Mount Rushmore?
4. Hustle, Gavotte, Fandango are all types of what?
5. Which star-sign falls between Libra and Sagittarius?
6. Why was the military kit known as the Sam Browne so called?
7. Is Zug — an area of Switzerland, an island off the coast of Belgium or a town in Ethiopia?
8. What does OHC refer to, on a car?
9. In backgammon, how many pieces does each player have?
10. Which cheese is recognisable by its covering of red wax?
11. Producer David O Selznick won best film Oscars for two classic movies. Name them?
12. What is toxicology the study of?
13. Would you find birds in an apiary or an aviary?
14. Is a mimbar — a hardwood tree, a pulpit in a mosque or a unit of pressure used in meteorology?
15. What is a polyglot able to do?
16. If a day is described as 'pluvial', what does this mean?

ANSWERS

1 A grapefruit, 2 40 years, 3 Washington, Jefferson, Lincoln, Roosevelt, 4 Dances, 5 Scorpio, 6 Named after Sir Sam Browne VC, who devised it to hold his sword and pistol, after he lost an arm, 7 An area of Switzerland, 8 Overhead camshaft, 9 15, 10 Edam, 11 Gone With The Wind (1939) and Rebecca (1940) , 12 Poisons, 13 An aviary, 14 A pulpit in a mosque, 15 Speak and write several languages, 16 It's a rainy day!

SPORT
Actively awesome!

1. What is the maximum number of clubs a golfer must carry in a competition?
2. How many balls are used in a game of billiards?
3. In boxing, the Manassa Mauler's real name was Jack Dempsey. True or false?
4. The term 'triangle and sausage' comes from which sport?
5. How many bases are in a game of baseball?
6. Tom Lehman and Fred Couples are both professional basketball players. True or false?
7. Who won the Tour de France in 2001?
8. In which year was the Ryder Cup first held in the United Kingdom?
9. How many Football League appearances did Peter Shilton make? 500, 800 or 1000?
10. Who won the Rugby League Challenge Cup in 1960? Warrington or Wakefield?
11. David Broome was a well-known name in which sport?
12. Which country won the FIFA World Cup in 1958, 1962 and 1970?
13. Is the Curtis Cup awarded for golf, tennis or rowing?
14. SCUBA is an acronym for what?
15. In football, who are the Blades?
16. From which wood is a cricket bat traditionally made?

ANSWERS

1 Fourteen, 2 Three, 3 True, 4 Yachting, 5 Four, 6 False. They are golfers, 7 Lance Armstrong, 8 1929, 9 1000, 10 Wakefield, 11 Show-jumping, 12 Brazil, 13 Golf, 14 Self-Contained Underwater Breathing Apparatus, 15 Sheffield United, 16 Willow.

KIDS' STUFF
Practically playtime!

1. Rachel Stevens was a member of which band?
2. Which long-distance walk starts in Milngavie, Glasgow, and ends up at Fort William?
3. In which movie would you find the Cowardly Lion and two different witches?
4. What is the alternative name for the Wardens of the Tower of London?
5. What was Frenchman Louis Bleriot's claim to fame?
6. What is Harry Potter's house called at Hogwarts School?
7. Which board game is also known as Alfapet, Skip-A-Cross and Funworder?
8. Which is the lowest-pitched string instrument?
9. Ka, Escort and Fiesta are models of cars manufactured by which company?
10. In which Scottish Region would you find the glens of Clova, Isla and Prosen?
11. In which city is the TV detective programme *Taggart* set? Edinburgh, Glasgow or Aberdeen?
12. Balti, Dupiaza and Korma are foods from which country?
13. In which fictional town is *The Simpsons* set?
14. Where is the popular holiday island of Madeira? The Mediterranean or the Atlantic?
15. What was the capital of China, Beijing, formally known as?
16. What are the names of the two children in the well-known story of *Chitty Chitty Bang Bang?*

ANSWERS

1 S Club 7, 2 The West Highland Way, 3 The Wizard of Oz, 4 Beefeaters, 5 He was the first man to fly over the English Channel, 6 Gryffindor, 7 Scrabble, 8 The double bass, 9 Ford, 10 Angus, 11 Glasgow, 12 India, 13 Springfield, 14 The North Atlantic, 15 Peking, 16 Jeremy and Jemima.

GENERAL KNOWLEDGE

How much do YOU know?

1. Is a Wahoo a North American Indian, a North African rug or a type of fish?
2. The wine, Marsalla, comes from where? Australia, Sicily, Malta or Argentina?
3. What is the diameter of a 2p piece?
4. In chess, what is the difference between a rook and a castle?
5. Which British army rank follows major, in seniority?
6. On a pencil, what do the letters HB mean?
7. This word can be a gardening aid, or an ancient burial mound — what is the word?
8. What was a 48k Spectrum, in the 1980s?
9. Which letter is second from the right on the top row of a normal keyboard?
10. If you are a campanologist, what is your hobby?
11. What is the unofficial name for Gravelly Hill Interchange near Birmingham?
12. Does dunlin mean — a fine-woven cloth, a small wading bird or the refuse of molten metal?
13. Where would you find treads and risers close together?
14. Aberdeen-Angus cattle are usually what colour?
15. Who were Sepoys?
16. What would you do with a quatrain?

ANSWERS

1 A type of fish, 2 Sicily, 3 2.5cm, 4 They are the same piece, 5 Lieutenant-Colonel, 6 Hard Black, 7 Barrow, 8 An early computer, the size of a small book, invented by Sir Clive Sinclair, 9 O, 10 Bell-ringing, 11 Spaghetti Junction, 12 A small wading bird, 13 On a staircase, 14 Black, 15 Indian soldiers in the British Army, 16 Recite it — it's a four-line poem.

THE SUNDAY POST FAMILY QUIZ BOOK

GENERAL KNOWLEDGE

Facts are fun!

1. In Roman numerals it is LXIV — how would we write it?
2. Is a Wandering Sailor a plant, a sewing style or a skin disease?
3. What is dried in an oast house?
4. If someone enjoys cartophily, what is their hobby?
5. Is a pedalo a Spanish sandal, a kind of boat or a brass musical instrument?
6. What number is on the opposite face to a three on a dice?
7. True or false — the highest value letters in the game of Scrabble are K and Q?
8. What is stored in a bodega?
9. How many great-great grandparents does the average person have?
10. Integral and differential are two forms of what?
11. What was a sedan chair?
12. In Greek mythology, who abducted Helen?
13. In the Army, what is an RSM?
14. What is psychokinesis?
15. Why do we have synchromesh in a car?
16. Whose motto is 'Blood And Fire'?

ANSWERS

1 64, 2 A plant, 3 Hops, 4 Collecting cigarette cards, 5 A small boat, 6 4, 7 False — it's Q and Z, 8 Wine, 9 Sixteen, 10 Calculus, 11 An early type of wheel-less transport, 12 Paris, 13 Regimental Sergeant-Major, 14 The power to move objects from a distance, using your mind, 15 It ensures that gear wheels engage smoothly, 16 The Salvation Army.

The SUNDAY POST FAMILY QUIZ BOOK

ENTERTAINMENT
Test your celebrity rating.

1. For how long did Bryan Adams' song, *Ev'rything I Do, I Do It For You*, top the charts in 1991?
2. What did John Bunyan write in Bedford jail?
3. Which gangster movie starred only children, no adults?
4. Who played Harry Lime in the classic film, *The Third Man?*
5. 'Nice to see you, to see you, nice!' is a catchphrase used by which TV personality?
6. Deuteronomy, Skimbleshanks and Growltiger appear in which musical?
7. Who or what was *Moby Dick?*
8. In the children's song, what was the name of Yankee Doodle's pony?
9. Errol Brown used to be lead singer in which band?
10. Rab C Nesbitt was played by whom on television?
11. The films *Home Alone* and *Home Alone 2* starred which young American actor?
12. What do Anne Howe, Britt Ekland, Miranda Quarry and Lynne Frederick have in common?
13. *The Lady Of Shalott* was a poem written by Keats, Coleridge or Tennyson?
14. What was unusual about *The Ballad Of Davy Crockett*, a song from 1956?
15. What is the name of the pub in TV's *Emmerdale?*
16. Can you name the singer who had a hit in 1969 with *Where Do You Go To, My Lovely?*

ANSWERS

1 Sixteen weeks, 2 Pilgrim's Progress, 3 Bugsy Malone, 4 Orson Welles, 5 Bruce Forsyth, 6 Cats, 7 A great white whale, 8 Macaroni, 9 Hot Chocolate, 10 Gregor Fisher, 11 Macaulay Caulkin, 12 They were all married to actor Peter Sellers, 13 Tennyson, 14 Four different artistes took the same song into the Top Thirty in the same year, 15 The Woolpack, 16 Peter Sarstedt.

GENERAL KNOWLEDGE

How much do YOU know?

● 1-5 Know a little! ● 6-11 Know a lot! ● 12-16 Know it all!

1. Nipper the dog appears on which music company logo?
2. If you went to see a trichologist what aspect of your health would you be concerned about?
3. What is a gnomon on a sundial?
4. Who played *Popeye* in the film of the cartoon?
5. Why is someone who is out of control and dangerous often called a 'loose cannon'?
6. Novelist George Orwell, comedian Spike Milligan and singer Sir Cliff Richard were all born in which country?
7. In the popular song, what comes after 'If I were a carpenter and you were a lady'?
8. The following are clues to Biblical characters: a) Tom Jones song, b) Elton John song, c) baby basket.
9. Myanmar in south-east Asia was formerly known as what?
10. What's the most worrying part of a guitar?
11. Which elephants have the bigger ears — African or Indian?
12. Can you think of a Cornish resort made up of one consonant and three vowels?
13. Who is the Queen's second oldest grandchild?
14. Can you get a suntan in a conservatory?
15. Rearrange ELBOW LOOP TRACK to identify a famous British holiday resort landmark.
16. According to the saying, who always blames his tools?

ANSWERS

1 HMV, 2 Your hair and scalp, 3 The bit that indicates the time by its shadow, 4 Robin Williams, 5 Cannons on ships had to be firmly secured because a heavy loose cannon could do a lot of damage, 6 India, 7 Would you marry me anyway, would you have my baby, 8 a) Delilah, b) Daniel, c) Moses, 9 Burma, 10 The frets, 11 African, 12 Looe, 13 Zara Phillips, 14 Probably not, as glass cuts out most of the radiation, 15 Blackpool Tower, 16 A bad workman.

GENERAL KNOWLEDGE

Take the test.

1. Where in a theatre is the parterre?
2. Does Gruyerre cheese have holes in it?
3. What is seriography?
4. Where would you find a coping stone?
5. A frontispiece is commonly found where?
6. On what common object might you find a welt, vamp and upper?
7. An optimistic buyer is known by what nickname in the Stock Exchange?
8. In law, primogeniture means a certain family member inherits an estate. Which one?
9. If an aircraft is described as STOL what does this mean?
10. If your hobby is lapidary what might you be doing?
11. When is St Patrick's Day?
12. What is 'cursive' writing?
13. Would you sit in, pull or wear a boater?
14. When was the 50p coin introduced?
15. How many pawns are there in a game of chess?
16. What type of worker may suffer from silicosis?

ANSWERS

1 The pit, 2 Yes, 3 Another name for silk-screen printing, 4 On the top of a wall, 5 In a book. It's an illustration facing the title page, 6 A shoe, 7 A bull, 8 The firstborn son, 9 Short Take-Off and Landing, 10 Polishing small stones for use in jewellery, 11 March 17th, 12 Writing done without lifting the pen, so the letters are joined, 13 Wear it — it's a hat, 14 1969, 15 Sixteen, 16 Miners or stone-workers.

GENERAL KNOWLEDGE
Facts are fun!

1. What was the name of the first American First Lady — Margaret, Martha, Mary or Marlene?
2. Duke of Rothesay, Earl of Carrick, Baron Renfrew and Lord of the Isles are whose titles?
3. How many individual cubes make up a Rubik's cube?
4. When was the Highway Code introduced — 1921, 1931 or 1941?
5. Name the first ship to respond to the distress call of the *Titanic*?
6. Which literary genius wrote, 'The female of the species is more deadly than the male'?
7. Is Wellington, the capital of New Zealand, on North or South Island?
8. In Greek mythology, who was Calliope?
9. Sesquicentennial refers to what?
10. Name the pop band who threw water over then Deputy Prime Minister John Prescott at the Brit Awards in 1998 — Culture Club, Chumbawamba or Sigue Sigue Sputnik?
11. If you suffer from anuptaphobia are you afraid of — opinions, garlic, staying single or men?
12. Name the cafe in the long-running US sitcom, *Friends*.
13. Where is the longest pier in Britain?
14. Name the first British footballer to break the £1 million transfer fee barrier.
15. Who was the first British sovereign to live in Buckingham Palace?
16. When did Lassie make her big screen debut — 1936, 1940, 1943 or 1946?

ANSWERS

1 Martha Dandridge Custis, George Washington's wife, 2 Prince Charles, 3 26, 4 1931, 5 *The Carpathia*, 6 Rudyard Kipling, 7 North, 8 Muse of Epic Poetry, 9 A 150th anniversary, 10 Chumbawumba, 11 Staying single, 12 Central Perk, 13 Southend, 14 Trevor Francis, in February, 1979, 15 Queen Victoria, 16 1943, in Lassie Come Home.

THE SUNDAY POST
FAMILY
QUIZ BOOK

GENERAL KNOWLEDGE

Quite quizzical!

1. Can you think of a type of seal with the same name as a musical instrument?
2. 'Suffering succotash' is the frustrated cry of which popular cartoon character?
3. What is an Emeritus professor?
4. Who performed with pop group Spandau Ballet before becoming an *EastEnders* resident?
5. Make a connection between Aunty Wainwright and *Coronation Street*.
6. Unscramble CASH RAN HAIR SALE to unveil the name of a TV actress.
7. What year saw the abolition of National Service in Britain — 1956, 1960 or 1964?
8. According to the rhyme, on which day was Solomon Grundy born?
9. Cover point is a position played in which sport?
10. In which sport do players hit a puck?
11. Which 1960s group is something you see when the sun shines?
12. Can you think of four slang expressions for a sleep?
13. What colours are in a Cornish flag?
14. A tangelo is a hybrid of which two other fruits?
15. What does your GP mean by RSI?
16. Americans call it a pacifier, but by what name do we know it?

ANSWERS

1 A harp seal, 2 Sylvester the Cat, 3 It's an honorary title for a professor who has retired, 4 Martin Kemp, 5 Aunty Wainwright was a character in Last Of The Summer Wine, played by Jean Alexander, who was Hilda Ogden in The Street, 6 Sarah Lancashire, 7 1960, 8 Monday, 9 Cricket, 10 Ice hockey, 11 The Shadows, 12 Nap, kip, snooze, forty winks, doze etc, 13 Black with a white cross, 14 Tangerine and pomelo, a fruit similar to a grapefruit, 15 Repetitive Strain Injury, 16 A baby's dummy.

ENTERTAINMENT
Totally TV.

1. This actor played the title roles in *Ironside* and *Perry Mason*. Who was he?
2. What's the connection between ITV's *Heartbeat* and Basil Brush?
3. This classic TV series was set in Walmington-On-Sea. Name the series.
4. In the 1950s children's TV programme *Rag, Tag And Bobtail,* which was the hedgehog?
5. Which fictional aliens come from the planet Skaro, and were the enemies of a mysterious Doctor?
6. When did Channel 4 begin broadcasting?
7. Which comedy series of the 1970s and 1980s introduced us to Miss Brahms and Mrs Slocombe?
8. In which fictional town would you find TV's *Coronation Street*?
9. 'You'll like it — not a lot!' was a famous catch-phrase of which TV personality?
10. Where is the Golden Rose television festival held annually?
11. Parker and Lady Penelope were characters from which children's TV series?
12. In the classic American TV comedy of that name, what did M.A.S.H. stand for?
13. Who played the title roles in the old TV series, *Starsky and Hutch*?
14. When did *Top Of The Pops* begin on BBC TV?
15. What was the full name of the character played by Penelope Keith in the comedy series *To The Manor Born*?
16. The American comedy *Cheers* was set in which city — Los Angeles, Boston or Washington?

ANSWERS

1 Raymond Burr, 2 Derek Fowlds (Oscar Blaketon in *Heartbeat* and Basil Brush's straight man in the 1970s), 3 Dad's Army, 4 Rag, 5 The Daleks, 6 1982, 7 Are You Being Served?, 8 Weatherfield, 9 Magician Paul Daniels, 10 Montreux, Switzerland, 11 *Thunderbirds*, 12 Mobile Army Surgical Hospital, 13 David Soul, Paul Michael Glaser, 14 1963, 15 Audrey fforbes-Hamilton, 16 Boston.

ENTERTAINMENT

Are you a star solver?

1. Who were the two female stars of the film *Whatever Happened To Baby Jane?*
2. *Dancing In The Dark, Born In The USA, Hungry Heart* — name the singer.
3. According to the nursery rhyme where, specifically, did the lamb follow Mary?
4. Was it Marie, Donny or Jimmy Osmond who had a hit in the 1970s with *Paper Roses?*
5. Who wrote the novel *Tinker, Tailor, Soldier, Spy?*
6. In Cribbage, how many points are scored for each '15' a player holds in his or her hand?
7. Can you name the three best pals of *Oor Wullie* in *The Sunday Post?*
8. Which actor's films include *Cool Hand Luke, Hud* and *The Hustler?*
9. Which dance requires the participant to wriggle under a low bar?
10. What is the highest number on a roulette wheel?
11. Chessboards and draughtsboards have a different number of squares — true or false?
12. Who played Pop Larkin in the TV drama series *The Darling Buds Of May?*
13. Name the group who had a massive hit with *Ride A White Swan* in 1970.
14. Which of these paintings was not the work of Vincent van Gogh? *The Potato Eaters, Sunflowers* or *The Madonna of the Rocks?*
15. Who sculpted *The Thinker?*
16. In the film of the same name, what is *The African Queen?*

ANSWERS

1 Bette Davis and Joan Crawford, 2 Bruce Springsteen, 3 To school, 4 Marie Osmond, 5 John Le Carré, 6 Two, 7 Fat Bob, Soapy Soutar, Wee Eck, 8 Paul Newman, 9 Limbo dancing, 10 36, 11 False — both games are played on the same board, 12 David Jason, 13 T-Rex, 14 Madonna of the Rocks is by Leonardo da Vinci, 15 Rodin, 16 A boat.

GENERAL KNOWLEDGE

Facts are fun!

1. The Grand Vitara is a model of car from Vauxhall, Ford or Suzuki?
2. Which wire on a domestic plug is green and yellow in colour?
3. Are millefiori ornaments made of brass, clay or glass?
4. What connects the Arabic, Mandarin and Hebrew languages?
5. Which grain is used in the production of malt whisky?
6. What is the basic difference between slander and libel?
7. Which of the forces would you find at Cranwell?
8. Who is reputed to have invented the vacuum flask?
9. A Bloody Mary cocktail is made from which ingredients?
10. How many points of the compass are there?
11. Apart from in a field, where would you be likely to find poppyheads?
12. Is a sidewinder a fishing-rod, a snake or a sewing stitch?
13. What is the best-known product of California's Napa Valley?
14. Where would you find *The Fool, Death* and *The Wheel Of Fortune*?
15. What's the difference between clavichord and clavicle?
16. A perforation gauge may be used in which hobby?

ANSWERS

1 Suzuki, 2 The Earth wire, 3 Glass, 4 They're all written right to left, 5 Barley, 6 Slander is spoken, libel is written, 7 It's an RAF training college, 8 James Dewar, 9 Vodka, tomato juice, Worcester sauce, 10 32, 11 Carvings on the ends of church pews, 12 A snake, 13 Wine, 14 In a pack of Tarot cards, 15 Clavichord is a musical instrument, clavicle is the collar-bone, 16 Stamp collecting.

GENERAL KNOWLEDGE

Quite quizzical!

1. True or false — epsilon is the sixth letter of the Greek alphabet?
2. The Bodleian Library is part of which university? St Andrews, Oxford or Cambridge?
3. What is meant by palimpsest?
4. What is a 'broken spectre'?
5. The wattle is the national flower for which country?
6. What is the seat of government of the Netherlands called?
7. At which university did Prince Charles read archaeology and anthropology?
8. In America, what is a stevedore?
9. Carob is used as a health-conscious substitute for what popular sweet tasting product?
10. What lines are marked TF, F, T, SW and WNA?
11. What are the main ingredients of Tia Maria liqueur?
12. Architecturally, what is a caryatid?
13. If a stamp has 'Suomi' on it, which country is it from?
14. If you and your friends have a hat, car, ship, iron, boot and dog, what are you doing?
15. How many lines are in a sonnet — eight, twelve or fourteen?
16. A tourniquet is used for what purpose?

ANSWERS

1 False — it's the fifth, 2 Oxford, 3 A manuscript on which the original writing has been removed to make room for other writing, 4 The magnified shadow of a person, cast onto a bank of fog or cloud in the mountains, 5 Australia, 6 The Hague, 7 Cambridge, 8 A person who loads and unloads ships, 9 Chocolate, 10 Load lines on a ship, 11 Coffee and rum, 12 A pillar or support carved in the shape of a draped female figure, 13 Finland, 14 Playing Monopoly, 15 14, 16 Stopping blood pumping from an artery that's been cut or damaged.

GENERAL KNOWLEDGE
How much do YOU know?

1. What world famous place remained closed for 3000 years until February 1923?
2. Which zodiac sign is represented by a set of scales?
3. What kind of creature is an addax?
4. Where would you see the abbreviation AOCB?
5. If you saw a dovetail but no feathers, what would you most likely be looking at?
6. Does a dormer window sit upright or on the slope of the roof?
7. 0141 is the telephone code for which city?
8. How deep is a fathom?
9. Is rococo a Latin-American big band sound, a pasta dish or a style of decoration?
10. How many quires make a ream, in paper measures?
11. Zander, Charr and Rudd are well-known figures in the fashion world — true or false?
12. If a clock in a mirror shows the time as ten minutes to four, what time is it in fact?
13. What was the fore-runner of the Royal Air Force?
14. 'Clunk, click, every trip' was an advertising slogan for what safety device?
15. Which motorway connects Bristol and London?
16. In a pack of cards, which is the only king shown in profile?

ANSWERS

1 Tutankhamun's tomb, 2 Libra, 3 An antelope, 4 In the minutes of a business meeting — it stands for Any Other Competent Business, 5 A carpentry joint, 6 Upright, 7 Glasgow, 8 1.8 metres, 9 A style of decoration, 10 Twenty, 11 False — they are freshwater fish, 12 Ten past eight, 13 The Royal Flying Corps, 14 Car seat belts, 15 The M4, 16 The King of Diamonds.

GENERAL KNOWLEDGE

Take the test.

● 1-5 Must try harder! ● 6-11 Could do better! ● 12-16 Top of the class!

1. What do you call the knife carried by Ghurka soldiers?
2. What would you be served if you ordered langoustine from a menu?
3. Is a fosse a trench, the base of a column or a sandwich?
4. How far would you go if you travelled a league on land?
5. What colour is the ribbon on the Victoria Cross?
6. Where might you find the motto, 'e pluribus unum'?
7. When was the Red Cross Organisation formed?
8. You'll find these in a set of bagpipes or a beehive — what are they?
9. From where did Tesco supermarket get its name?
10. If you are parsimonious, are you generous or mean?
11. At the festival of Up-Helly-A what gets burnt?
12. How is milk pasteurised?
13. In Morse Code, which letter is indicated by a single dash?
14. Which post-war comedian used the catch-phrase 'Hello, Playmates!'?
15. Was a hogshead equivalent to 50, 75 or 100 gallons?
16. Polled cattle are unusual in one particular way. What is it?

ANSWERS

1 The kukri, 2 Lobster, 3 A trench, 4 About three miles, 5 Crimson, 6 On American coinage. It means 'one out of many', 7 1864, in Geneva, 8 Drones, 9 From TE Stockwell and Jack Cohen, 10 Mean, 11 A facsimile of a Viking longboat, 12 By heating it to a temperature of about 62 degrees C then maintaining that temperature for half an hour, 13 The letter 'T', 14 Arthur Askey, 15 50, 16 They have been deprived of their horns.

THE SUNDAY POST FAMILY QUIZ BOOK

GENERAL KNOWLEDGE

How much do YOU know?

1. Wine is made from grapes, but what is tequila made from?
2. What object can be divided into four cantons?
3. If someone is described as gravid, are they heavy-handed, pregnant or rough-voiced?
4. When was the Ordnance Survey, the state department for the mapping of Britain, established?
5. A quadrille is a square dance for how many couples?
6. If you are at a butcher's shop, and ask for a bit of skirt, what would you get?
7. If you take a size 8 shoe in Britain, what is the equivalent size in the rest of Europe?
8. Which is not an Army rank — Santiago, Bogota, Lima, Colombo?
9. Brigadier, Major-General, Group-Captain, Lieutenant-Colonel — which is the odd one out?
10. In which month do Americans celebrate Thanksgiving Day?
11. Do horse-drawn carriages require a Road Fund Licence?
12. What tradesman might use gripper?
13. What is the day before Ash Wednesday known as?
14. With traffic signs, what shape are the ones on which instructions are given?
15. What is semantics?
16. Centrepin and fixed spool are types of what?

ANSWERS

1 Cactus, 2 A flag, 3 Pregnant, 4 1791, 5 Four, 6 Meat from the lower flank or diaphragm of an animal, 7 42, 8 Colombo — all the others are in South America 9 Group-Captain, it's an RAF rank, not Army, 10 November, 11 No, 12 A carpet-layer. It's the edging which holds fitted carpets in place, 13 Shrove Tuesday, 14 Circular, 15 The meaning of words, 16 Fishing reels.

The Sunday Post
FAMILY QUIZ BOOK

GENERAL KNOWLEDGE

Take the test.

1. Which member of the Royal Family was born on the eighth day of the eighth month in 1988?
2. Which Ayrshire town gives its name to a willow tree?
3. What, when bought new, comes with a NHBC 10-year guarantee?
4. Who took over from Betty Boothroyd as House of Commons Speaker?
5. Where is the Gulf of Bothnis?
6. What, technically, is a dowager?
7. Who played the ghost in the original TV series *Randall & Hopkirk?*
8. 'The minute you let her under your skin, Then you begin to make it better' are lines from which Beatles recording?
9. If you booked a holiday to Cancun you'd be going to which country?
10. Which famous literary figure had a son called Hamnet?
11. Why is a top pupil called a dux?
12. If Alpha is the first Greek letter, what's the fourth?
13. Is limnology the study of limbs and muscles, citrus fruit, cloud formations or lakes and freshwater basins?
14. In parts of England they call them barm cakes. How do people refer to them in Scotland?
15. Which car company shares its name with a bridge in London?
16. Why is an articulated lorry so called?

ANSWERS

1 Princess Beatrice, 2 Kilmarnock, 3 A house, it's the National House-Building Council, 4 Michael Martin, 5 In the northern Baltic, between Sweden and Finland, 6 The widow of an earl or count. The title distinguishes her from the wife of her late husband's heir, 7 Kenneth Cope, who played Marty Hopkirk, 8 Hey Jude, 9 Mexico, 10 William Shakespeare, 11 It's the Latin word for leader, 12 Delta, 13 Lakes and freshwater basins, 14 As rolls, 15 Vauxhall, 16 Articulated means jointed and the cab can move at an angle to the rear section.

SPORT
Play a part!

1. Is Sergio Garcia a footballer, athlete or golfer?
2. The Jules Rimet Trophy was awarded for speedway riding, cycling or football?
3. True or false — Sheffield Wednesday's nickname is the Owls?
4. Where might the Red Lichties come from?
5. Which northern Rugby Union side are known as the Falcons?
6. Which Scottish football team are known as the Bully Wee?
7. Richard Corsie was a champion in which sport?
8. Who was the Isle Of Man TT Champion for three years running in the 1960s?
9. Which American tennis star was often called Superbrat?
10. On a dartboard, which number comes after 16, going clockwise?
11. Graham Gooch is a name associated with which sport?
12. Which Japanese martial art's name translates as 'gentle way'?
13. What sport is played at Cowdray Park?
14. What is the distance between the goalposts in a professional game of football?
15. In Rugby Union, when was the four-point try introduced?
16. When was the Davis Cup first competed? 1888, 1900 or 1908?

ANSWERS

1 Golfer, 2 Football, 3 True, 4 Arbroath, 5 Newcastle, 6 Clyde, 7 Bowling, 8 Mike Hailwood, 9 John McEnroe, 10 Eight, 11 Cricket, 12 Judo, 13 Polo, 14 Eight yards (7.32 metres), 15 1972, 16 1900.

GENERAL KNOWLEDGE

How much do YOU know?

1. The Gotland Islands in the Baltic Sea belong to which country?
2. Can you think of four places in the UK beginning with a bird?
3. What does 'exercising your franchise' mean?
4. From which English football club did Sam Allardyce resign as manager, just before the end of season 2006-2007?
5. Who set up the British Astrological and Psychic Society — Patrick Moore, Russell Grant, Jonathan Cainer or Uri Geller?
6. Which British army commander was nicknamed 'Old Nosey'?
7. Which is the highest mountain in the Alps? Mont Blanc or the Matterhorn?
8. Who or what are the Dodecanese?
9. What was the mythological Greek river that separated Earth from the Underworld?
10. If a lintel is above a door what's below?
11. What's unusual about a Blenheim Orange?
12. Aconcagua is the highest mountain in South America. Which country is it in?
13. Who was US President at the dawn of the 20th Century — William McKinley, Theodore Roosevelt or Woodrow Wilson?
14. Why is something honest or legitimate 'above board'?
15. For how long may a golfer search for a ball before it's declared lost?
16. If you had a 'Scotch Argus' in your garden what would you be looking at?

ANSWERS

BRAINBOX
The Body Beautiful!

● 1-5 At the foot! ● 6-11 A little waist! ● 12-16 Well ahead!

1. Is the tragus part of your eye, ear or stomach?
2. How many muscles are in the human body — around 320, 530 or 640?
3. Where in the human body is the sternum?
4. What is produced by the lacrymal gland?
5. Blepharitis is inflammation of which part of the body?
6. What is the average area of skin on a human body? 10, 20 or 30 square feet?
7. Is the hallux a bone in your neck, shoulder or foot?
8. What name is given to the fibre which joins muscle to bone?
9. What is the decibel level of normal speech?
10. Which has two X chromosomes, male or female?
11. Where would you find Fourth Gutter and Palace of Weariness?
12. Which part of your body might suffer from nystagmus — the ears, the eyes or the toes?
13. If your body shape is described as endomorph are you round, lean or rectangular?
14. What is the soft spot on a new baby's head called?
15. What do you call a cavity in the skin which holds a hair root?
16. What is the outer layer of skin on the human body called?

ANSWERS

1 It's the flap at the entrance to your ear, 2 Around 640, 3 In the chest, 4 Tears, 5 The eye, 6 20 square feet, 7 Foot, it's your big toe, 8 Tendon, 9 45 to 55 decibels, 10 Female, 11 On your body — they are acupuncture points, 12 Your eyes — it's rapid, involuntary movement of the eyeballs, 13 round, 14 The fontanelle, 15 Follicle, 16 Epidermis.

The SUNDAY POST FAMILY QUIZ BOOK

GENERAL KNOWLEDGE

Take the test.

1. In the Peter Sellers and Sophia Loren song, which lyric precedes 'Well, goodness gracious me'?
2. A 'knot' is the collective noun for a group of squirrels, lizards, turtles or toads?
3. 'You too can have a body like mine' was a quote by whom?
4. The title of a book by David Baddiel is the same as the catchphrase used by *The Magic Roundabout's* Zebedee. What is it?
5. What's the main difference between glass and crystal?
6. How many faces does a dodecahedron have?
7. Your heart has how many chambers?
8. What does 'philharmonic' in an orchestra's title mean?
9. At which battle was King James the Fourth of Scotland killed?
10. Actor Peter Lawford was the brother-in-law of which US president?
11. What can be a motorcycle attachment or a cocktail?
12. Which creamy dessert takes its name from a world famous Russian ballerina?
13. In 1950 the world's first credit card was introduced. Was it a Diners Club, Mastercard, American Express card or a Barclaycard?
14. Where in your body is the labyrinth?
15. According to the TV ad 'Top breeders recommend it'. What is the product?
16. What were Hoovervilles in the USA in the 1930s?

ANSWERS

1 Oh Doctor I'm in Trouble, 2 Toads, 3 Bodybuilder Charles Atlas, 4 Time For Bed, 5 Crystal contains lead, 6 Twelve, 7 Four, 8 Fond of music or loving harmony, 9 Flodden, 10 John F Kennedy, 11 A sidecar, 12 Pavlova, from Anna Pavlova, 13 Diners Club, 14 In your inner ear, 15 Pedigree Chum, 16 Shanty towns for unemployed workers, named after President Herbert Hoover.

GENERAL KNOWLEDGE

Take the test.

1. If you intend to keep a vehicle off the road for a while you should fill in a SORN form. What do the letters indicate?
2. Black, White, Green, Brown and Scarlet are the surnames of people in what?
3. Who's missing from *Friends* — Rachel, Ross, Monica, Chandler and Joey.
4. In the rhyme what did the sparrow claim to have killed Cock Robin with?
5. What do the initials of a CD ROM stand for?
6. Rearrange NO STREAM HAT to recall a tale by Robert Burns.
7. Driving a Ulysses would you be behind the wheel of a Fiat, Ford, Mitsubishi or Honda?
8. Which Angus town is built on a basin?
9. What's the connection between Captain Cook's ship and Inspector Morse?
10. We've all heard of the Moulin Rouge in Paris, but what does it mean in English?
11. Which European capital city is built on seven hills?
12. How many faces has an icosahedron — 12,16,18 or 20?
13. Max Factor of make-up fame was an American immigrant from where?
14. Which of TV's *The Goodies* is now known as an ornithologist?
15. Which member of the Royal Family is President of the National Playing Fields Association — Princess Anne, Prince Edward, Prince Andrew or Prince Philip?
16. Is Gardener's Delight a type of carrot, lettuce, tomato or radish?

ANSWERS

1 Statutory Off Road Notification, 2 The board game Cluedo, 3 Phoebe, 4 His bow and arrow, 5 Compact Disc Read Only Memory, 6 Tam O'Shanter, 7 Fiat, 8 Montrose. It's a sea inlet, 9 Both were called Endeavour, 10 Red windmill, 11 Rome, 12 20, 13 Russia, 14 Bill Oddie, 15 Prince Philip, 16 Tomato.

ENTERTAINMENT
Are you a star solver?

1. What was the name of the actress who starred in the 1930s film *King Kong?*
2. Who wrote about Tom Sawyer and Huckleberry Finn?
3. In 1991 Cher hit the No.1 spot with a very oddly-titled song. What was it?
4. Who played Damien in TV's classic comedy series *Drop The Dead Donkey?*
5. Name the presenter of the series of performing foul-ups on TV called *It'll Be Alright On The Night.*
6. Was the composer Bartok Austrian, Hungarian or Dutch?
7. In the story of *The Wizard Of Oz* by L Frank Baum, what is the Tin Man's name? Hickory, Dickory or Dock?
8. Which band had a hit with *Why Does It Always Rain On Me?*
9. The castle of Elsinore features in which Shakespeare play?
10. What was the heroine's profession in the musical film and stage show *South Pacific?*
11. What was Betamax?
12. The play *Shirley Valentine* was written by Ben Elton, Tom Stoppard or Willy Russell?
13. Superman, as Clark Kent, works for which newspaper?
14. Who was the original host of TV's *The Price Is Right?*
15. Name the famous British actor who wrote a book entitled *Bring On The Empty Horses?*
16. Who had consecutive hits with *Stand By Your Man* and *D.I.V.O.R.C.E.?*

ANSWERS

1 Fay Wray, 2 Mark Twain, 3 The Shoop Shoop Song, 4 Stephen Tompkinson, 5 Dennis Norden, 6 Hungarian, 7 Hickory, 8 Travis, 9 Hamlet, 10 Navy nurse, 11 A former standard for video recording, 12 Willy Russell, 13 The Daily Planet, 14 Leslie Crowther, 15 David Niven, 16 Tammy Wynette.

ENTERTAINMENT
Are you a star solver?

1. The film *Three Coins In A Fountain* is associated with which fountain?
2. How old was writer Ernest Hemingway when he died — 58, 61 or 64?
3. In a waltz tune how many beats are in a bar?
4. What was Tom Jones's first hit?
5. *10 Rillington Place* was a film about which murderer?
6. *The Ride Of The Valkyries* is a musical composition by Verdi, Vivaldi or Wagner?
7. If you are a philumenist, what do you collect?
8. The novel by HG Wells, *War Of The Worlds,* was published in 1898, 1904 or 1913?
9. Which group won the Eurovision Song Contest in 1981?
10. Who played the son in the classic sitcom *Steptoe and Son?*
11. Would you blow, hit or strum the instrument known as an ocarina?
12. Who played Dr Hugo Hackenbush in the film *A Day At The Races?*
13. Finish the name of Edward Albec's well-known play. *Who's Afraid Of _____?*
14. Can you give the first names of the singing duo of the 1950s and 1960s, The Everly Brothers?
15. Calypso music originated where?
16. In *A Midsummer Night's Dream* who casts a spell on Titania?

ANSWERS

GENERAL KNOWLEDGE

Facts are fun!

1. Name any three arch-enemies of 007 in James Bond films.
2. Why do we call an experienced seaman an 'old salt'?
3. Who was Bobby Ewing's brother-in-law and JR's arch enemy in the US show *Dallas*?
4. Can you think of three girl's names that are also letters of the alphabet?
5. Why do we say it's raining cats and dogs?
6. According to the title of the famous Betty Smith book, where does a tree grow?
7. If you landed at Rhoose Airport would you be in Canada, Nigeria or Wales?
8. Why do we refer to the toilet as 'the loo'?
9. Which entertainer used a wobble board as a musical instrument?
10. Which of our senses is used least every day?
11. What do you call the shortest distance between two points?
12. Which comes first — thunder or lightning?
13. What prolific romantic author penned the Mallen series of books?
14. What's the most commonly used expression in the world?
15. In the musical film *On The Town*, were the lead characters soldiers or sailors?
16. Why do we use the expression 'to pass the buck'?

ANSWERS

1 Dr Julius No, Ernst Stavro Blofeld, Francisco Scaramanga, Auric Goldfinger, Hugo Drax etc, 2 Because he has been well salted by the sea, 3 Cliff Barnes, 4 Dee, Kay, Bea, Elle etc, 5 Strays often drowned in poorly-drained streets of old, which led people to use the expression, 6 Brooklyn, 7 Wales, it's Cardiff airport, 8 Probably a corruption of l'eau, French for water, 9 Rolf Harris, 10 Taste, 11 A straight line, 12 Lightning, 13 Catherine Cookson, 14 Okay, 15 Sailors, 16 The buck was a knife used by poker players and passed around to indicate whose turn it was to play.

THE SUNDAY POST
FAMILY
QUIZ BOOK

GENERAL KNOWLEDGE
Quite quizzical!

1. When a car tyre is worn down in the middle and like new at the edges, is it a sign that it's over or under-inflated?
2. Name the first proper programme to go out on Channel 5 when it began on March 30, 1997.
3. Which island is furthest west — Colonsay, Islay or Jura?
4. In what year was *Blue Peter* first televised — 1958, 1960 or 1962?
5. Can you think of a sauce named after a Mexican state?
6. Short statements of wisdom, this is also a book of The Bible. Name it.
7. Is amontillado something to drink, a burrowing mammal, a slimline cigar or a tropical storm?
8. Eric Arthur Blair wrote under which pen name?
9. Which North African city's name translates from the Spanish meaning 'white house'?
10. According to the Book of Joshua, the walls of which city came down at the sound of trumpets?
11. Unscramble PIN MY GOAL to find a well-known George Bernard Shaw play.
12. Clarence Nash provided the voice for which cartoon character — Elmer Fudd, Foghorn Leghorn, Mickey Mouse or Donald Duck?
13. Lake Bala is the largest lake in which country?
14. What does ETD on a transport timetable stand for?
15. What was Frank Sinatra's middle name?
16. Is a wimple something worn by a jockey, a nun, a cowboy or a scuba diver?

ANSWERS

1 Over-inflated, 2 Family Affairs, 3 Islay, 4 1958, 5 Tabasco, 6 Proverbs, 7 Something to drink. It's a pale dry sherry, 8 George Orwell, 9 Casablanca, 10 Jericho, 11 Pygmalion, 12 Donald Duck, 13 Wales, 14 Estimated Time of Departure, 15 Albert, 16 A nun — it's a type of headcloth.

THE SUNDAY POST
FAMILY
QUIZ BOOK

GENERAL KNOWLEDGE

How much do YOU know?

1. Which Derbyshire town is associated with a delicious almond flavoured pudding?
2. If you're served borscht in a restaurant what are you eating?
3. Which fictional superhero feared the substance kryptonite?
4. Cheviot, Shetland, Boreray, Hebridean and Orkney are all breeds of what?
5. *TISWAS* was a zany children's show starring Chris Tarrant. What did the acronym stand for?
6. Which university city is further south — Cambridge or Oxford?
7. Who was the original presenter of TV's *Stars In Their Eyes*?
8. Can you think of a board game with a type of meat in its name?
9. If paleology is the study of antiquities, what is paleontology the study of?
10. Which popular song by Boney M was about the slave trade from Africa to the USA?
11. If you saw a fritillary in the country would you have caught sight of a flower, a rock formation, a butterfly or a bird?
12. If a stylus is used to play records, what is used on compact discs?
13. The Tramontana is a feature of Mediterranean countries. What is it?
14. If you're in Eilat, which country are you in?
15. Mensa is an organisation for people of a high IQ. What does the name mean?
16. *Close Every Door To Me* is a song from which popular musical?

ANSWERS

1 *Bakewell*, 2 *Soup made with beetroot and/or cabbage*, 3 *Superman*, 4 *Sheep*, 5 *Today Is Saturday Wear A Smile*, 6 *Oxford*, 7 *Leslie Crowther*, 8 *Backgammon*, 9 *Fossils of plants and animals, often dinosaurs*, 10 *Rivers Of Babylon*, 11 *A butterfly*, 12 *A laser beam*, 13 *A cold north wind from the mountains*, 14 *Israel*, 15 *From mens, the Latin for mind*, 16 *Joseph and the Amazing Technicolor Dreamcoat.*

GENERAL KNOWLEDGE

Take the test.

● 1-5 Must try harder! ● 6-11 Could do better! ● 12-16 Top of the class!

1. Which of Henry VIII's wives had 11 fingers?
2. What does the W stand for in George W Bush?
3. How is the depressive illness SAD otherwise known?
4. What was *George and Mildred's* surname in the popular TV sitcom?
5. Whose treasure is buried on RL Stevenson's Treasure Island?
6. We've probably all heard of the Pentland Skerries, but what exactly are skerries?
7. Which of the following abbreviations won't you see in a lonely-hearts ad: a) WLTM, b) TLC, c) GSOH, d) BLT?
8. Which famous cartoon character is known as Topolino in Italy?
9. Why might you see arrows on your hotel room ceiling in Malaysia?
10. What type of Indian cookery takes its name from the type of oven it's cooked in?
11. What word can follow snake, Bible and seat?
12. Unscramble LONDON'S SAVERS to recall a DH Lawrence title.
13. St Crispin is the patron saint of which clothing trade?
14. What drink's name is derived from the Spanish word for bleeding?
15. How many Emirates make up the United Arab Emirates?
16. Would you wear, lie on or climb with a 'futon'?

SPORT
Play a part!

1. England cricketer Ian Botham played for which professional football team?
2. What is Tic Tac?
3. During a game, how many players are on a basketball court at the same time?
4. In cricket, what is a maiden over?
5. Is Venus Williams a javelin-thrower, synchronised swimmer or tennis player?
6. How does a cricket umpire signal a bye?
7. How many throwing events are there in a Decathlon?
8. What is ledger fishing?
9. On leaving Manchester United, which football team did Roy Keane sign for in 2005?
10. In which sport is there a yokozuna?
11. How many players are there in a netball team?
12. With which sport do you associate the term 'yorker'?
13. Snooker player James Wattana comes from which country? Hong Kong, Thailand or Korea?
14. In flat green bowling, what is the minimum distance that a bowler can throw the jack?
15. How many foot-faults can the server in tennis have, before losing a point?
16. With which sport would you associate the terms prime, quart and octave?

ANSWERS
---

1 Scunthorpe United, 2 Bookmakers' sign language on a racecourse, 3 Ten, 4 When no runs are scored, 5 Tennis player, 6 By raising an open hand above his head, 7 Three — shot put, discus and javelin, 8 Fishing with weights but no float on the line, 9 Celtic, 10 Sumo Wrestling, 11 Seven, 12 Cricket: it's a ball thrown to bounce under the batsman's bat, 13 Thailand, 14 25 yards, 15 Two, 16 Fencing.

SPORT
True or false – you say which.

1. Ex-boxer Lennox Lewis was born in Canada.
2. Tennis players Andy and Jamie Murray are both left-handed.
3. Snooker's Stephen Hendry was born in Paisley.
4. The 'road hole bunker' is at the 17th hole of the Old Course at St Andrews.
5. A tennis net must be 1.07m high at the posts.
6. 'Round the Clock', 'Cricket' and 'Killer' are all games of darts.
7. An Olympic swimming pool must be no more than 25m long.
8. Badminton was launched in 1873 at Badminton House.
9. A high jump bar is usually made from balsa wood.
10. The London Marathon was first held in 1981.
11. Squash was recently dropped as an Olympic sport.
12. Kelly Holmes won gold in the 200m and 400m at the 2004 Olympics.
13. Phil 'the Power' Taylor is associated with weightlifting.
14. Pitroddie is the home ground of Aberdeen FC.
15. Diego Maradona's 'Hand of God' goal against England was scored in the 1986 World Cup.
16. Legendary Australian cricketer, Don Bradman, scored over 7000 test runs.

ANSWERS

1 False, he was born in London, 2 False, Andy is right-handed, 3 False, South Queensferry, 4 True, 5 True, 6 True, 7 False, it should be 50m, 8 True, 9 False, it's normally aluminium or plastic, 10 True, 11 False, it hasn't yet been included, 12 False, it was 800m and 1500m, 13 False, he's a darts player, 14 False, it's Pittodrie, 15 True, 16 False, he scored 6996.

GENERAL KNOWLEDGE
Facts are fun!

1. Why do we say something is squeaky clean?
2. Which of the following is a French bagpipe — a bayette, chantette, dronette or a musette?
3. Which member of the Royal Family has the other names Albert Christian Edward?
4. The 60th anniversary of John Lennon's birth was marked by the opening of a museum, but is it in Liverpool, New York or Tokyo?
5. Is howtowdie a chicken recipe, a ball game or a ghostly apparition?
6. In Arthurian legend, what was the Holy Grail?
7. Rearrange HAIL SMART CHANT to find a gardening presenter.
8. Elvis Presley, Marlene Dietrich and Jack Warner starred in films with blue in the title. Name the films.
9. What was the relationship between *Winnie The Pooh* author AA Milne and Christopher Robin?
10. In rhyming slang, what are your saucepans?
11. Which county doesn't have a coast — Angus, Lanarkshire or Fife?
12. What Perthshire town has a namesake in the Falkland Islands?
13. Which artist learned about the workings of the human body by dissecting corpses?
14. Which of these Beatles film was a cartoon — *Help!, A Hard Day's Night* or *Yellow Submarine?*
15. What word can refer to both blood and a monkey?
16. In business, what do the letters SGM stand for?

ANSWERS
---

1 From newly-washed hair which is so clean it squeaks, 2 A musette, 3 Prince Andrew, 4 Tokyo, 5 A chicken recipe, 6 The cup from which Christ drank at the Last Supper, 7 Alan Titchmarsh, 8 Blue Hawaii, The Blue Angel, The Blue Lamp, 9 Father and son, 10 Children, from saucepan lids, kids, 11 Lanarkshire, 12 Stanley, 13 Leonardo da Vinci, 14 Yellow Submarine, 15 Rhesus, 16 Special General Meeting.

GENERAL KNOWLEDGE
Quite quizzical!

1. In which soap opera do villagers live in the fictional county of Borsetshire?
2. What plantlife inspired Swiss engineer Georges de Mestral, the inventor of Velcro?
3. According to the children's rhyme, which day's child is supposed to be loving and giving?
4. Louise Nurding was formerly a member of which all-girl singing group?
5. Who was seven times World Snooker Champion during the 1990s?
6. Name the largest member of the dolphin family.
7. Both are celebrated in July, but does Canada Day fall before or after American Independence Day?
8. Who produces hit musicals through the Really Useful Group?
9. Name the longest motorway in the UK.
10. Where in an old house could you find an inglenook?
11. In military terms what does NCO stand for?
12. Name the northernmost nation on the continent of Europe.
13. 2000 in Roman numerals is written as MM. What is 1900 in Roman numerals?
14. Finish off this Monty Python catchphrase, 'And now for _____'
15. Which six-letter word can precede envelope, seat and cleaner?
16. The word claret refers to red wine from which region of France?

ANSWERS

1 *The Archers*, 2 *Sticky plant burrs, which cling to your clothes when you brush past the plant*, 3 *Friday's child*, 4 *Eternal*, 5 *Stephen Hendry*, 6 *The killer whale*, 7 *Three days before, on July 1*, 8 *Sir Andrew Lloyd Webber*, 9 *The M6 at 199.3 miles*, 10 *By the fireside. It's a small recess or corner by a fireplace*, 11 *Non-commissioned officer*, 12 *Norway*, 13 *MCM*, 14 *Something completely different*, 15 *Window*, 16 *Bordeaux*.

THE SUNDAY POST FAMILY QUIZ BOOK

ENTERTAINMENT
Test your celebrity rating.

1. Whose smile remained even after the character disappeared in *Alice In Wonderland?*
2. In what year was Slim Whitman's *Rose Marie* a smash hit — 1955, 1956 or 1957?
3. The 1980s comedy series *Just Good Friends* starred Paul Nicholas as Vince, but who played Penny?
4. What was the subject of the book and film *Papillon?*
5. His films include *Paint Your Wagon, Cat Ballou* and *The Killers.* Who is this actor?
6. Who wrote the set of musical pieces known as *The Planets Suite?*
7. Was Long John Silver a character in *Treasure Island, Coral Island* or *Kidnapped?*
8. In Shakespeare's *A Midsummer Night's Dream* what other name is given to Puck?
9. Which Scottish writer died in Samoa?
10. In the 1977 BBC drama *The Onedin Line* who played the role of James Onedin?
11. Name three actors who have been *Batman* on film.
12. Who was the young diary-writer in the popular books by Sue Townsend?
13. When did Luciano Pavarotti reach No.2 in the charts with *Nessun Dorma* — 1990, 1991 or 1992?
14. Who was the star of *Knight Rider?*
15. What was the name of Georgie Fame's backing group in the 1960s?
16. How many Oscars did the film *One Flew Over The Cuckoo's Nest* win in 1975?

ANSWERS

1 The Cheshire Cat, 2 1955, 3 Jan Francis, 4 A French convict escaping from the penal colony known as Devil's Island, 5 Lee Marvin, 6 Holst, 7 Treasure Island, 8 Robin Goodfellow, 9 Robert Louis Stevenson, 10 Peter Gilmore, 11 Val Kilmer, George Clooney, Michael Keaton, 12 Adrian Mole, 13 1990, 14 David Hasselhoff, 15 The Blue Flames, 16 Five.

ENTERTAINMENT
Test your celebrity rating.

1. In an orchestra, what would a flautist be doing?
2. Claude Monet, Edouard Manet, Henri Menet. Which was not a famous artist?
3. Name the type of vehicle which starred in the film *Speed*.
4. How many black keys are there on a standard piano — 27, 32, 35, or 39?
5. In the film *Casablanca* which song was Sam asked to play?
6. When did Fred Astaire die — 1983, 1985 or 1987?
7. In the James Bond books, what was the name of the company used as cover for the spy's activities?
8. Which poet wrote 'If I should die, think only this of me.'?
9. What number completes the book title _____ Leagues Under The Sea?
10. Which singer used to be known as The Little Sparrow?
11. What was John Travolta's character's name in *Saturday Night Fever?*
12. In which book might you meet a rabbit called Fiver?
13. Valerie Tatlock, Janet Reid, Deirdre Langton — what's the connection?
14. True or false — Kajagoogoo had a Top Ten hit in 1983 with *Ooh To Be Ah?*
15. Who was responsible for the theme music for the film *Chariots Of Fire?*
16. In which pantomime does a crocodile feature?

=== ANSWERS ===

1 *Playing a flute*, 2 *Henri Menet*, 3 *A bus*, 4 *35*, 5 *As Time Goes By*, 6 *1987*, 7 *Universal Exports*, 8 *Rupert Brooke*, 9 *20,000*, 10 *Edith Piaf*, 11 *Tony Manero*, 12 *Watership Down*, 13 *They've all been married to Ken Barlow, in Coronation Street*, 14 *True*, 15 *Vangelis*, 16 *Peter Pan*.

GENERAL KNOWLEDGE

How much do YOU know?

1. What type of headgear is named after a Crimean battle?
2. Name three Shakespeare plays beginning with M.
3. What's the proper name for marsh gas?
4. *Offside* is the theme tune for which popular BBC TV programme?
5. At what sport did Britain win its first gold medal at the 2000 Olympics?
6. How tall is ex-Premier Tony Blair?
7. Clyde Barrow's middle name was Champion, Capability or Conqueror?
8. Which has more rooms — Buckingham Palace or the White House?
9. What's the name of: a) the police station in Heartbeat, b) the fire station in London's Burning?
10. What's the link between singers Tom Jones, Shirley Bassey and Charlotte Church?
11. Which Scottish football team are known as the Hoops and why?
12. Name three London airports.
13. How old do you have to be to qualify for a free TV licence — 65, 70 or 75?
14. What would you not be able to do if you suffered from aphonia — dance, chew, play the piano or speak?
15. A famous spy called Margarete Gertrude Zelle was better known as who?
16. Name three actors who have played Hamlet in film versions of the play.

ANSWERS

1 Balaclava, 2 Macbeth, Measure For Measure and Much Ado About Nothing, 3 Ethane, 4 Match Of The Day, 5 Cycling, 6 Six feet, 7 Champion, 8 Buckingham Palace with over 600. The White House has 132 rooms, 9 a) Ashfordly Police Station, b) Blackwall Fire Station, 10 They are all Welsh, 11 Glasgow Celtic, because of the green hoops on their jerseys, 12 Gatwick, Stansted, Heathrow, London City or Luton, 13 75, 14 Speak — it's loss of voice, 15 Mata Hari, 16 Any three from Laurence Olivier, Mel Gibson, Kenneth Branagh, Nicol Williamson, Richard Burton.

GENERAL KNOWLEDGE

Take the test.

1. Which animal used to be known as a camelopard?
2. Do South African motorists drive on the left or right of the road?
3. Why are the days of your youth known as your salad days?
4. What nationality is singer Shania Twain?
5. What is a gilt on a farm?
6. Why are stiletto heels so called?
7. What fruit is a cross between a plum and a peach?
8. Jim Smith changed his name before becoming famous in *Carry On* films. Name him.
9. DVT is a condition that sometimes affects people on long haul flights. What does it stand for?
10. In which country is Constantia Wine made? France, Chile, South Africa or New Zealand?
11. Served in an Indian restaurant, unleavened spiced bread made from ground lentils and fried in oil is called what?
12. What's unusual about a polydactyl person?
13. Name any four musical instruments in the woodwind family.
14. When might loudspeakers remind you of dogs and birds?
15. Unscramble RICH SOLAR WIND to find a popular Scottish actor.
16. Which British city lies on the same line of latitude as the Russian capital city of Moscow?

ANSWERS

1 The giraffe, 2 The left side, 3 Because you are fresh, green and youthful like a crisp newly-made salad, 4 Canadian, 5 A young female pig, 6 Stiletto is an Italian word for a small dagger to which the heels were likened, 7 The nectarine, 8 Jim Dale, 9 Deep vein thrombosis, 10 South Africa, 11 A poppadom, 12 They have more than five digits on their hands and feet, 13 Flute, oboe, clarinet, bassoon, piccolo, saxophone etc, 14 When they have woofers and tweeters, 15 Richard Wilson, 16 Edinburgh.

BRAINBOX

For smarties only!

1. Which Apollo Moon Mission was a near-disaster for the astronauts?
2. If you are 'au fait' with something, do you know it well, are you carrying it or are you right next to it?
3. An angle of less than 90 degrees is known as what?
4. If something is referred to as isotropic, what does this mean?
5. What is your tarsus?
6. How are disease organisms carried by house-flies?
7. Which substance has the chemical symbol Pu?
8. When an object in space is at its perihelion, where is it?
9. What is the meaning of 'itis' in words like arthritis, bronchitis, appendicitis?
10. We've all heard of DNA, but what exactly do the letters stand for?
11. Name Scotland's second-highest mountain?
12. Which metal is the best conductor of electricity?
13. What does a hydrologist study?
14. Who or what is a shaman?
15. A Kelvin is a measurement — but of what?
16. What can anaerobic organisms live without?

ANSWERS

1 Apollo 13, 2 You are well-acquainted with it, 3 An acute angle, 4 Having the same physical properties in all directions, 5 Your ankle, 6 On the hairs of their legs, 7 Plutonium, 8 The object is at its closest point to the Sun, 9 Inflammation, 10 Deoxyribonucleic acid, 11 Ben Macdui, 12 Silver, 13 Water resources in the world's land areas, 14 A 'medicine man' who uses magical arts to cure, 15 Temperature, 16 Oxygen.

GENERAL KNOWLEDGE
How much do YOU know?

1. Why do we speak about doing something in the 'nick of time'?
2. The following answers contain the word 'bag': a) old board game, b) French loaf, c) *Jungle Book* panther.
3. What do the initials NASA stand for?
4. Pick the odd one out — Lupo, Golf, Lancer, Polo, Sharan.
5. Do ostriches really bury their heads in the sand?
6. If you ordered 'misket' in a restaurant what would the waiter bring?
7. In light entertainment, what's the difference between a duo and a duet?
8. Which successful 1960s singing group were originally known as The Primettes?
9. If you win something hands-down it requires little effort. Why hands-down?
10. The infamous highwayman Dick Turpin lived in which century?
11. Which dance step comes from a French word meaning 'spinning top'?
12. Who wrote the music to the ballet *Sleeping Beauty*?
13. Name *The Three Musketeers*.
14. Does a piano belong to the string or percussion section of an orchestra?
15. What military rank did Lawrence of Arabia hold?
16. Who wrote the music to *Rule Britannia*?

ANSWERS

1 A nick was a narrow, precise marker to indicate the passing of time, so something 'in the nick' was exactly where it should be, 2 a) bagatelle, b) baguette c) Bagheera, 3 National Aeronautics and Space Administration, 4 Lancer is a Mitsubishi. The others are Volkswagens, 5 No, but they do lie down with their necks flat on the ground to make themselves less conspicuous, 6 A Bulgarian wine, 7 A duo is a two-person musical act. A duet is a song sung by two people, 8 The Supremes, 9 When they were approaching the finishing line with no other riders near them, jockeys would relax and put their hands down, 10 18th, 11 Pirouette, 12 Tchaikovsky, 13 Athos, Porthos and Aramis, 14 Percussion, 15 Lieutenant-Colonel, 16 Thomas Arne.

GENERAL KNOWLEDGE

Take the test.

1. According to superstition, how many magpies mean a secret?
2. Most gardeners have used John Innes compost, but who was John Innes?
3. Unscramble CHEAP BLAME to identify a tatsty item on a dessert menu.
4. Who spoke the first words in the first episode of the TV soap *EastEnders*?
5. St Andrew is the patron saint of Scotland, Greece and where else — Russia, Belgium or Canada?
6. Which composer wrote symphonies entitled *Paris* and *Prague*?
7. Which US President delivered the Gettysburg Address?
8. Where and what is the Menin Gate?
9. When was the Battle of the Alamo?
10. In which range of mountains would you find the Inaccessible Pinnacle?
11. Laser, Mirror and Devon Lugger are all types of which sort of craft?
12. Former US President Bill Clinton plays which musical instrument?
13. Name the second largest Balearic island.
14. Was Davy Crockett a real or fictitious person?
15. Is Leeds Castle in Yorkshire, Kent or Lancashire?
16. Which volcano is situated on Sicily? Mount Etna or Mount Vesuvius?

■ ANSWERS ■

1 Seven, 2 A 19th Century Londoner who gave a lot of money to gardening research, 3 *Peach melba*, 4 Den Watts, played by Leslie Grantham, 5 Russia, 6 Mozart, 7 Abraham Lincoln, 8 Ypres, Belgium. It is a memorial to the fallen of World War One, 9 1836, 10 The Cuillins, Skye, 11 Dinghies, 12 Saxophone, 13 Minorca, 14 Real. He was an American frontiersman and politician who died at the Battle of the Alamo, 15 Kent, 16 Mount Etna.

KIDS' STUFF
Practically playtime!

1. In which county is Alton Towers?
2. Who was the voice behind *Bob the Builder*?
3. *Dennis the Menace* appears in which children's comic?
4. Name the very famous toy store in London's Regent Street.
5. What sort of creature is *Pingu*?
6. From which Scottish city does the band The View come? Edinburgh or Dundee?
7. Who was Madonna's second husband?
8. Which river flows through York? The Ouse or the Humber?
9. What is the capital of Sweden?
10. Which country borders Switzerland on its eastern side?
11. Who wrote *Treasure Island*?
12. Who played the part of Captain Jack Sparrow in the film *Pirates of the Caribbean*?
13. What is the connection between Peter Davison, Christopher Eccleston and David Tennant?
14. In which series of films would you find Hobbits and Orcs?
15. What is significant about London's Pudding Lane?
16. True or false — Robin Hood's adventures took place near the city of Bath?

ANSWERS

1 Staffordshire, 2 Neil Morrisey, 3 The Beano, 4 Hamley's, 5 A penguin, 6 Dundee, 7 Guy Ritchie, 8 The Ouse, 9 Stockholm, 10 Austria, 11 Robert Louis Stevenson, 12 Johnny Depp, 13 They have all played the part of Doctor Who, 14 Lord of the Rings, 15 It was where the Great Fire of London started, 16 False. They took place near Nottingham.

GENERAL KNOWLEDGE

Facts are fun!

1. What were the full names of Messrs Rolls and Royce of motor car fame?
2. Where are your ilium bones?
3. If you're acrophobic what do you fear?
4. In Cockney rhyming slang, what's a syrup of fig?
5. Which TV advert used the slogan, 'Full of Eastern promise'?
6. Which village in Fife shares its name with the Roman goddess of grain?
7. What's the origin of the word laser?
8. How long have you been married when you celebrate your Tin Wedding Anniversary?
9. In mythology who are the Amazons?
10. Name three ailments which have been named after an occupation or activity.
11. Why is the Equator so called?
12. Which Dickens character gave her name to a large umbrella?
13. In which year was the Battle of Trafalgar?
14. Which composer was known as 'The Father of the Symphony'? Handel, Holst or Haydn?
15. In which US state is New Orleans?
16. Which actor appeared with Kathleen Turner in the movie *Romancing The Stone*?

ANSWERS

1 Charles Stewart Rolls and Frederick Henry Royce, 2 In your pelvis, 3 Great heights, 4 A wig, 5 Fry's Turkish Delight, 6 Ceres, 7 From the initials of Light Amplification by Stimulated Emission of Radiation, 8 10 years, 9 A race of female warriors, 10 Any four from Athlete's foot, tennis elbow, housemaid's knee, writer's cramp etc, 11 From equate, meaning equal, because it's of equal distance from both poles, 12 Sarah Gamp, 13 1805, 14 Haydn, 15 Louisiana, 16 Michael Douglas.

THE SUNDAY POST
FAMILY
QUIZ BOOK

GENERAL KNOWLEDGE
Quite quizzical!

1. Solve the following clues to James Bond characters: a) peculiar task, b) shiny digit, c) they bite.
2. What are a cat's vibrissae?
3. Unscramble LINEN ENVY GLEE to reveal the name of a famous Scottish musician.
4. What purpose do our olfactory organs serve?
5. Of which English football club is TV chef Delia Smith a great fan and shareholder?
6. According to the rhyme, which child is full of grace?
7. Mullets were all the rage in the 1980s. What were they?
8. Which 20th Century US President had the middle name Earl?
9. Which body is famous for the motto 'My Word Is My Bond'?
10. Are there more left-handed men or women?
11. Which French Marshal promised he'd capture Napoleon and bring him home in an iron cage?
12. Which famous German composer wrote the *Kreutzer Sonata* for violin and piano?
13. What is the capital city of Croatia?
14. True or false — the Caspian Sea feeds into the Mediterranean Sea?
15. What, in France, is an 'arrondissement'?
16. Who were Alan, Les, Derek, Stuart and Eric in the 1970s?

ANSWERS

1 a) Oddjob, b) Goldfinger, c) Jaws, 2 Its whiskers, 3 Evelyn Glennie, 4 They give us our sense of smell, 5 Norwich City, 6 Tuesday's child, 7 Gents' hairstyles cut fairly short on top, cropped at the sides and left long at the back, 8 Jimmy Carter, 9 The London Stock Exchange, 10 There are more left-handed men, 11 Marshal Ney, 12 Beethoven, 13 Zagreb, 14 False. It's land-locked, 15 An administration division of a city, 16 The Bay City Rollers.

GENERAL KNOWLEDGE

How much do YOU know?

1. What can be cold, ginger or a popular card game?
2. The border between Scotland and England stretches for how many miles — 98, 108, 118 or 128?
3. In 1960 *Dreadnought* became Britain's first what?
4. On a French restaurant menu, the word veronique denotes a dish, usually chicken or fish, garnished with what?
5. Does the honey bee have one, three, five or seven eyes?
6. What do Americans call a guide dog for the blind?
7. Cambozola cheese comes from which European country?
8. What was the name of the explorer who sailed on a ship called the *Santa Maria?*
9. Which Gilbert and Sullivan operetta is also know as *The Slave of Duty?*
10. Where is the Isle de la Cite?
11. Who composed the *Radetzky March?*
12. The French had the Maginot Line, but what was the German equivalent?
13. Which river flows through Berlin?
14. Who sang *A Man's A Man For A' That* at the Scottish Parliament opening ceremony in 1999?
15. What do the queens hold in their hands in a pack of playing cards?
16. Which fruity sounding Spanish city is the capital of the region of Andalucia?

ANSWERS

1 Snap, 2 108 miles, 3 Nuclear submarine, 4 Grapes, 5 They have five eyes, 6 A seeing-eye dog, 7 Germany, 8 Christopher Columbus, 9 The Pirates of Penzance, 10 Paris, 11 Johann Strauss, 12 The Siegfried Line, 13 The Spree, 14 Sheena Wellington, 15 A flower, 16 Seville.

GENERAL KNOWLEDGE

Take the test.

1. What can be an alcoholic drink, a biscuit and a European royal family?
2. What is a grandad on a shirt?
3. After the sun, which is the closest star to Earth — Vega, Proxima Centauri, Betelgeuse or Altair?
4. Identify the following fictional bears: a) London railway station, b) Nutwood resident, c) *Jungle Book* star.
5. Did Sherlock Holmes really exist?
6. Can the world's tallest hedge be found in Scotland, England, Japan or the USA?
7. What type of cake is broonie?
8. What does Regis in Bognor Regis mean?
9. Who sang the theme to the 1967 Sidney Poitier film *To Sir With Love?*
10. Which opera does the famous aria *Your Tiny Hand Is Frozen* come from?
11. Who was known as the Queen of The Music Hall?
12. Which planet is orbited by a moon named Ganymede?
13. What do Michael Caine and Jude Law have in common?
14. Where would you be most likely to encounter a kinkajou?
15. In which Dickens novel would you find the Marquis St Evermonde and Madame Defarge?
16. Should real tennis be played on an indoor or outdoor court?

ANSWERS

1 Bourbon, 2 A style of collar, 3 Proxima Centauri, also known as Alpha Centauri C, 4 a) Paddington, b) Rupert, c) Balloo, 5 No. Arthur Conan Doyle created him, 6 Scotland. *The Beech Hedge* at Meikleour, Perthshire, reaches 36.6m (120 ft), 7 Gingerbread, 8 Of the king, 9 Lulu, 10 La Bohème, 11 Marie Lloyd, 12 Jupiter, 13 They both played the title roles in the film Alfie, 14 In a zoo or the rainforests of Mexico, Central and South America. It's a nocturnal mammal, 15 A Tale of Two Cities, 16 An indoor court.

GENERAL KNOWLEDGE

Facts are fun!

1. Why is it impossible to play the card game Canasta with a pack of standard playing cards?
2. Which American honour bears the inscription 'For Military Merit'?
3. What does AM on a radio dial stand for?
4. What was 2LO in the 1920s?
5. In Scottish folklore, what is a kelpie?
6. Is raw steak really the best remedy for a black eye?
7. Light sabres were weapons used in which famous film?
8. Is myology the study of blood cells, explosives, muscles or minerals?
9. Rearrange GO THEN A DEFENDER to discover a Biblical location.
10. Which name is a type of grass — Timothy, Terence, Thomas or Troy?
11. Which five instruments perform Schubert's *Trout Quintet*?
12. The Battle of Bunker Hill took place during which war?
13. Which country has a greater land mass — China or the USA?
14. When did the first Butlins camp open — 1928, 1932, 1936 or 1939?
15. What are the letters Q and Z worth in Scrabble?
16. Samuel Sebastian Wesley is remembered for his contribution to what?

■ **ANSWERS** ■

1 Because you need two packs, 2 The Purple Heart, 3 Amplitude Modulation, 4 The first transmitter used by the BBC, 5 A water spirit, 6 No, it's no more effective than a moist cloth or sponge, 7 Star Wars, 8 Muscles, 9 The Garden of Eden, 10 Timothy, 11 Piano, violin, viola, cello and double bass, 12 American War of Independence, 13 China, 14 1936, 15 They're both worth 10 points, 16 Composing anthems and hymns.

THE SUNDAY POST
FAMILY
QUIZ BOOK

ENTERTAINMENT
Movie mania!

1. Name the star of the 1951 film, *Man In A White Suit*.
2. In the film *Goodbye Mr Chips*, what subject did he teach?
3. Who directed the following films — *Torn Curtain, Spellbound, Frenzy*?
4. What was the title of the follow-up film to John Travolta's *Saturday Night Fever*?
5. When did Fred Astaire die — 1983, 1985 or 1987?
6. In the film *Some Like It Hot* did Tony Curtis play trumpet, saxophone or trombone?
7. If an actor is said to 'go dry', what does this mean?
8. In the James Bond films, who was M's secretary?
9. The climax of the film *North By Northwest* takes place at which American landmark?
10. Who owned the Millennium Falcon in the *Star Wars* films?
11. True or false — the first film in Smell-O-Vision was released in 1968?
12. Who was the female lead in the 1961 film *Whistle Down The Wind*?
13. 'In space, no one can hear you scream' is from the advertising for which film?
14. How many Oscars did the film *Shakespeare In Love* win?
15. Ratso was a character played by Dustin Hoffman in which film opposite John Voigt?
16. How old was Elizabeth Taylor when she starred in the film *National Velvet*?

ANSWERS

ENTERTAINMENT
Test your celebrity rating.

1. Portia appears in which Shakespeare play?
2. In the classic film *Some Like It Hot* who played the part of Sugar Cane?
3. What was the Bay City Rollers' first No.1?
4. Who played the bumbling Spanish waiter in the TV comedy series *Fawlty Towers?*
5. What was the Rolling Stones' first hit record, back in 1963?
6. The *Jeeves* stories of PG Wodehouse were dramatised in the early 1990s, but who starred as the famous butler?
7. In the film *Fantastic Voyage* where does the journey take place?
8. Were the fictional detectives *Maigret* and *Poirot* of the same nationality?
9. Which instrument was Liberace best known for playing?
10. Flying Lizards, Flying Pickets, Flying Gnomes — which of these has not had a hit single?
11. Name Muriel Spark's famous novel about an Edinburgh teacher.
12. Into which section of an orchestra is the saxophone placed?
13. True or false — Humphrey Bogart did not win an Oscar for his part in *The African Queen?*
14. 'The evil that men do lives after them' is a quote from which Shakespeare play?
15. Who had a hit with *Da Doo Don Ron Ron* in 1963 — The Supremes, The Crystals or The Shirelles?
16. *Raindrops Keep Falling On My Head* was a hit song. But from which film did it come?

ANSWERS

1 *The Merchant of Venice*, 2 *Marilyn Monroe*, 3 *Bye Bye Baby*, 4 *Andrew Sachs*, 5 *Come On. It reached No.21 in the charts*, 6 *Stephen Fry*, 7 *Inside the human body*, 8 *No — Maigret was French, Poirot was Belgian*, 9 *The piano*, 10 *Flying Gnomes*, 11 *The Prime of Miss Jean Brodie*, 12 *The woodwind section*, 13 *False*, 14 *Julius Caesar*, 15 *The Crystals*, 16 *Butch Cassidy and the Sundance Kid*.

GENERAL KNOWLEDGE
Quite quizzical!

1. Which boy's name comes from the Greek meaning 'defender of men' — Thomas, Matthew, Alexander, Arthur?
2. Which former British colony is affectionately known as Honkers?
3. Q is a character in the James Bond films, but what does Q stand for?
4. When can oil wells be likened to teeth?
5. If quesadillas are on the menu, in what type of restaurant are you eating?
6. In which year did the communist dictator Stalin die?
7. By what name is the speedy animal 'Acinonyx jubatus' better known?
8. What is spelunking: a) playing truant from school, b) exploring caves, c) making cocktails, d) diving for shellfish?
9. Which singer found fame in the 1970s after changing his name from Gerard Hugh?
10. With which city are Wagner's *Meistersinger* associated?
11. Identify the following British postcodes: a) KY, b) BT, c) NE, d) ZE.
12. Join the symbols for the chemical elements calcium and iron together to find a place to go for a meal.
13. A Soviet minister for foreign affairs gave his name to which crude type of explosive?
14. What type of puppet begins with a girl's name?
15. At which castle was Mary, Queen of Scots beheaded?
16. 'Isca Dumnoniorum' was the Roman name for which English city?

ANSWERS

1 Alexander, 2 Hong Kong, 3 Quartermaster, 4 Because they can both be capped or drilled, 5 Mexican, 6 1953, 7 The cheetah, 8 Exploring caves, 9 Leo Sayer, 10 Nuremberg, 11 a) Kirkcaldy, b) Belfast, c) Newcastle-upon-Tyne, d) Shetland, 12 Café (CA & FE), 13 Molotov cocktail, from Vyacheslav Mikhailovich Molotov, 14 A marionette, 15 Fotheringay, 16 Exeter.

THE SUNDAY POST
FAMILY
QUIZ BOOK

BRAINBOX
For smarties only!

1. What disease nearly wiped out the rabbit population of Britain in the 1950s?
2. What chemical compound is the principal constituent of chalk?
3. What gas has the chemical symbol CH_4?
4. How many vertebrae are in the human neck - seven, nine or eleven?
5. What is a parsec?
6. Pulex Irritans is a parasitic insect, more commonly known as what?
7. Does the word 'auric' refer to gold, bronze or silver?
8. What is the maximum force on the Beaufort Scale?
9. Obstetrics is concerned with what type of care?
10. What is the term for electrical cable which has one conductor inside the other?
11. Laika was an animal that travelled into space in the 1950s. Was it a monkey, dog or chicken?
12. What term describes light rays bending as they pass through a lens?
13. Which is heavier — platinum or gold?
14. If you suffer from narcolepsy, what can't you help doing?
15. What is parkesine, and when was it invented?
16. What is the purpose of the spleen in the human body?

ANSWERS

1 Myxomatosis, 2 Calcium carbonate, 3 Methane, 4 Seven, 5 A unit of distance in astronomy equivalent to 19.2 million million miles, 6 The (human) flea, 7 Gold, 8 12, 9 Medical care during and after pregnancy, 10 Co-axial — like a television aerial cable, 11 Dog, 12 Refraction, 13 Platinum, 14 Falling asleep, 15 The first plastic, invented by Alexander Parkes, 16 It purifies the blood.

SPORT
Play a part!

1. If you went to Edgbaston, which sport would you probably be going to see?
2. Is a skeleton a fencing term, a small boat or a sledge?
3. Name two sports played with wooden mallets.
4. When was the first Grand National horse race? 1839, 1849 or 1859?
5. Who won four successive British Grand Prix from 1962 to 1965?
6. In boxing, what time-period is allowed between rounds?
7. What was Dundee United originally called?
8. When someone's job requires them to wear 'silks', what might their occupation be?
9. Was Nelson Piquet a football player, racing driver or jockey?
10. What is the width of the goals in water polo?
11. What is the height of the net in table tennis? Six, seven or eight inches?
12. From which country does the football team Benfica come — Italy, Spain or Portugal?
13. Which sport do you associate with the name Clare Wood?
14. Which three sports involve slaloms?
15. In ten-pin bowling, what is the maximum possible score in one game?
16. In which year did Arthur Ashe win the Men's Singles title at Wimbledon? 1975, 1976 or 1977?

ANSWERS

1 Cricket, 2 A sledge, 3 Polo and croquet, 4 1839, 5 Jim Clark, 6 One minute, 7 Dundee Hibernian, 8 A jockey, 9 Racing driver, 10 Three metres, 11 Six inches, 12 Portugal, 13 Tennis, 14 Skiing, water skiing and canoeing, 15 300, 16 1975.

GENERAL KNOWLEDGE

How much do YOU know?

1. Why is a tall dark male said to be a lucky first foot?
2. Can you think of a sugary cake topping with a large number name?
3. Was there really a Dick Whittington or is it just a story?
4. According to the *Harry Potter* novels which creatures run Gringotts, the wizards' bank?
5. What is tintinnabulation?
6. In JM Barrie's *Peter Pan* what is Wendy's surname?
7. What size precedes Private Eye to complete a Hanna-Barbera cartoon character?
8. What's the state capital of Georgia?
9. In Roman mythology is Pax the goddess of spring, peace, the harvest or love?
10. Crufts dog show is held annually in which British city?
11. Rearrange I'M A DOT IN PLACE to find something this phrase is describing.
12. Old Father Time is usually depicted as holding what kind of implement?
13. 'And the world is like an apple whirling silently in space' is a lyric from which 1969 recording?
14. Daley Thompson was an Olympic gold medalist in which athletics event?
15. The following clues are for 'inn' words: a) suggestive remark, b) public house host, c) bright idea, d) Austrian city.
16. According to the World War Two slogan, what did careless talk cost?

ANSWERS

1 It's thought to be from the days when Scots feared blond Viking raiders, 2 Hundreds and thousands, 3 The character is loosely based on Richard Whittington, a textile dealer who was Lord Mayor four times, 4 Goblins, 5 The ringing of bells, 6 Darling, 7 Inch High, 8 Atlanta, 9 Peace, 10 Birmingham, at the NEC, 11 A Decimal point, 12 A scythe, 13 The Windmills Of Your Mind, 14 Decathlon, 15 a) Innuendo, b) innkeeper, c) innovation, d) Innsbruck, 16 Lives.

GENERAL KNOWLEDGE

Take the test.

1. Which organisation uses the slogan 'Rise Above The Rest' in recruitment campaigns?
2. Percy, James, Toby and Edward are friends of which character?
3. Under what name did country singer Virginia Hensley find fame — Patsy Cline, Dolly Parton or Emmy-Lou Harris?
4. Which canal links the North Sea with the Baltic Sea?
5. St Magnus is the patron saint of which Scottish island?
6. The song *You'll Never Walk Alone* comes from which musical?
7. Identify these Clint Eastwood films: a) daub your truck, b) power to a champagne bottle, c) ghost-like horseman.
8. An odometer measures the distance covered by what?
9. What is a Grandee in Spain?
10. Which of the following comedians wasn't discovered on Opportunity Knocks — Frank Carson, Freddie Starr, Jim Davidson or Tom O'Connor?
11. What Australian soap actor/singer shares a name with a 1960s singer?
12. Who played Beatrix in the movie *Miss Potter*?
13. What is Maundy Money?
14. 'Mister Brown goes off to town on the eight twenty-one' is a line from which classic TV theme?
15. Who created the detective Maigret — Georges Simenon, Leslie Charteris or John Creasey?
16. James Short made his name as a Scottish comedian and entertainer after changing his name to what?

ANSWERS

THE SUNDAY POST

FAMILY

QUIZ BOOK

GENERAL KNOWLEDGE
Facts are fun!

● 1-5 Could improve! ● 6-11 Getting better! ● 12-16 The best!

1. Which five words are inscribed on the letterbox on the front of 10 Downing Street?
2. When was golfing champion Tiger Woods born — 1972, 1975 or 1978?
3. Which 1960 Hitchcock film begins with a secretary stealing $40,000?
4. Which 'foreign' building can be found at 24 Grosvenor Square, London?
5. If one's a wish and two's a kiss, what's three?
6. How did the expression 'back to square one' originate?
7. These clues give answers beginning with the name 'Ben': a) Hebridean island, b) fast-talking comedian, c) colourful clothing store.
8. When might a gentleman wear a potaine?
9. What features on the logo of the DVLA?
10. Which James Bond movie is also a breed of duck?
11. The sound holes on a violin resemble which letter of the alphabet?
12. What is a horse's withers?
13. Under what name did Mrs Darrell Waters become a children's author?
14. Which star sign covers the period March 20 to April 19?
15. What kind of bird do you mostly associate with Loch Garten?
16. Which Scottish island's name means 'kingdom under the waves' — Bute, Colonsay, Coll or Tiree?

ANSWERS

1 First Lord Of The Treasury, 2 1975, 3 Psycho, 4 The United States Embassy, 5 A back at square one, 6 From board games where players roll the dice and often end up disappointment, 7 a) Benbecula, b) Ben Elton, c) Benetton, 8 With a kilt. It's a sleeveless tunic worn over a loose-fitting shirt, 9 The initials on a triangle with a broken centre line representing a road, 10 Goldeneye, 11 The letter S. The second one is backwards, 12 The ridge at the base of the back of the neck, 13 Enid Blyton, 14 Aries, 15 The osprey, 16 Tiree.

ENTERTAINMENT

Are you a star solver?

● 1-5 Star gazing! ● 6-11 Star bright! ● 12-16 Starring role!

1. True or false — an orchestral tam-tam is a type of drum?
2. What was the name of the Bronte sisters' brother?
3. When was the Keanu Reeves movie *Speed* released — 1989, 1991 or 1994?
4. Which band had a No.1 hit in 1979 with I Don't Like Mondays?
5. Sean Connery won an Oscar for Best Supporting Actor for which film in 1987?
6. In Tennyson's poem, how many 'rode into the Valley of Death'?
7. Cathy McGowan presented this TV pop show in the 1960s. Can you name it?
8. Who played *Bergerac* on TV?
9. Was Jimmy Lea in the Yardbirds, Slade or Small Faces?
10. In which year were the remains of the Globe Theatre rediscovered?
11. Bruce Wayne and Clark Kent — can you name these characters' super-hero identities?
12. *Brown Girl In The Ring* was a hit for this group in April 1978. Who were they?
13. On a musical score, what do the letters pp mean?
14. Who wrote the poem *The Railway Bridge of the Silvery Tay*?
15. *Smokey And The Bandit* was a hit film for which actor?
16. In *The Sunday Post's Oor Wullie* story, what's the name of the policeman?

ANSWERS

1 False — it's a gong, 2 (Patrick) Branwell, 3 1994, 4 The Boomtown Rats, 5 The Untouchables, 6 Six hundred, 7 Ready Steady Go, 8 John Nettles, 9 Slade, 10 1989, 11 Batman and Superman, 12 Boney M, 13 Pianissimo — very soft, 14 William McGonagall, 15 Burt Reynolds, 16 PC Murdoch.

ENTERTAINMENT
Test your celebrity rating.

1. Name the author who created the villain Hannibal Lecter.
2. How many girls are there in the band known as the Corrs?
3. The 1951 film *Strangers On A Train* was the work of which world famous director?
4. Who wrote the novel Captain Corelli's Mandolin which was later made into a successful movie?
5. Norman Stanley Fletcher called himself what, in the classic comedy series *Porridge?*
6. Who composed the waltz known as *The Blue Danube?*
7. Felix, Korky, Rupert, Garfield — which of these cartoon characters is the odd one out?
8. Debbie Harry was lead singer with which 1980s band?
9. Richard Bacon, Mark Curry, Tim Rice — which was not a *Blue Peter* presenter?
10. The *Free Willy* films are concerned with which creature?
11. According to Shakespeare, whose ghost takes Macbeth's place at the banquet table?
12. In which pantomime tale will you find Never-Never Land?
13. Which unlikely duo had a No.1 hit with Ebony And Ivory back in the early 1980s?
14. Who was Clint Eastwood's unusual co-star in the film, *Every Which Way But Loose?*
15. The character Alf Garnett first appeared on our screens in 1965. But in which TV series?
16. Did Cliff Richard sing his hit song *Bachelor Boy* in the film *Summer Holiday?*

ANSWERS

1 Thomas Harris, 2 Three, 3 Alfred Hitchcock, 4 Louis de Bernieres, 5 A guest of Her Majesty — in other words, a prisoner in jail, 6 Johann Strauss, the younger, 7 Rupert — he's a bear, the others are cats, 8 Blondie, 9 Tim Rice, 10 Killer Whale (Orca), 11 Banquo's ghost, 12 Peter Pan, 13 Paul McCartney and Stevie Wonder, 14 Clyde, an orang-utan, 15 Till Death Us Do Part, 16 Yes.

ENTERTAINMENT
Test your celebrity rating.

1. How many pilgrims are in Chaucer's *Canterbury Tales* — 23, 29 or 31?
2. Keith Harris and Orville the Duck reached No. 4 in the Charts with *Orville's Song* in which year?
3. In the poem by Longfellow, by which river did Hiawatha live?
4. In the film *A Fistful Of Dollars* which character did Clint Eastwood play?
5. What was the original career of thriller writer Dick Francis?
6. What's the connection between Madonna, Michelle, Rita, Lucy and Eleanor?
7. Is a euphonium a brass or woodwind musical instrument?
8. The Stevie Wonder hit song *I Just Called To Say I Love You* was used in which film?
9. Which three colours combine to make a picture on television?
10. Name the deadly plants in the novel by John Wyndham.
11. Was the girls' comic *Bunty* first published in 1954, 1958 or 1962?
12. Which fictional character's address was Railway Cuttings, East Cheam?
13. In the film *Star Wars* who was Luke Skywalker's father?
14. Who founded the London Philharmonic Orchestra in 1932?
15. Hemmingway's *For Whom The Bell Tolls* is set in which era?
16. Who were the original publicans in *Coronation Street's* Rover's Return?

ANSWERS

The SUNDAY POST
FAMILY
QUIZ BOOK

GENERAL KNOWLEDGE

Fantastic firsts!

1. What first was achieved by Judith Keppel?
2. Name the first man to swim the English Channel.
3. Which actor played TV's first *Dr Who?*
4. What is the first event in a decathlon?
5. The first programme ever broadcast on Channel 4 is still running today. What is it?
6. What was Agatha Christie's first published novel?
7. Name the first wife of Henry VIII.
8. What is the first line of Wordsworth's famous poem, *The Daffodils?*
9. 'It is a truth universally acknowledged, that a single man in possession of a good fortune, must be in want of a wife' is the first sentence from which book?
10. What is the first song sung in the musical *Oklahoma?*
11. Who was Scotland's first First Minister?
12. Which US soap came first — *The Colbys* or *Dynasty?*
13. Who was tennis player Andre Agassi's first wife?
14. Which was the first TV soap in Britain — *Coronation Street, Emergency Ward 10, The Grove Family* or *The Forsyte Saga?*
15. The first popular music chart was published by American magazine *Billboard* in 1936, 1946 or 1956?
16. Louise Brown created a stir when she was born in 1978. Why?

ANSWERS

1 She was first to win £1 million on Who Wants To Be A Millionaire, 2 Captain Matthew Webb, 3 William Hartnell, from 1963-66, 4 The 100m, 5 Countdown, 6 The Mysterious Affair at Styles, 7 Catherine of Aragon, 8 I wandered lonely as a cloud, 9 Pride and Prejudice, 10 Oh, What a Beautiful Mornin', 11 Donald Dewar, 12 Dynasty, 13 Brooke Shields, 14 The Grove Family, which ran on BBC from 1954 to 1957, 15 1936, 16 She was the first test tube baby.

GENERAL KNOWLEDGE

How much do YOU know?

1. How is Marshall Mathers better known to pop fans?
2. How many wives of Henry VIII were called Catherine?
3. Unscramble NO BAN ON RESIN to reveal a TV quiz show host.
4. Is the moon approximately 125,000, 250,000 or 375,000 miles away from Earth?
5. How is the US game tic-tac-toe known to us?
6. Which fruit has seeds on the outside?
7. Served in an Italian restaurant, what type of food is mascarpone — ice cream, cheese, pasta or garlic bread?
8. Name the cartoon villain in *Wacky Races*.
9. American Milton Hershey founded a company making what?
10. The following are clues to dances: a) jumbled 60th of an hour, b) shaky insect, c) entwine.
11. What is the origin of the name of the Scottish rock band Runrig?
12. Which is a real place in Sutherland — Teeth, Earlobe, Nose or Tongue?
13. Name three US states beginning with 'M'.
14. What's unusual about a butterfly's feet?
15. Name the baker in the card game Happy Families.
16. Name the two male leads in the film *White Christmas*.

ANSWERS

1 As rapper Eminem, 2 Three. Catherine Howard and Catherine Parr, 3 Anne Robinson, 4 About 250,000 miles, 5 As noughts and crosses, 6 The strawberry, 7 It's a soft, mild cream cheese, 8 Dick Dastardly, 9 Chocolate products, 10 a) Minuet, b) jitterbug, c) twist, 11 Runrig was the name for a system whereby land was split into strips and apportioned in rotation each year to tenant farmers, 12 Tongue, 13 Any three from Maryland, Maine, Michigan, Missouri, Montana etc, 14 They have tiny cells on them with which the insect can taste its food, 15 Mr Bun, 16 Bing Crosby and Danny Kaye.

GENERAL KNOWLEDGE

Take the test.

1. What is a Gatso at the roadside?
2. Arrange the following Scottish bridges from north to south —
   Friarton Bridge, Erskine Bridge, Kessock Bridge, Kincardine Bridge.
3. Deely boppers were a silly fashion accessory of the 1980s. Where did you wear them?
4. Which Volkswagen car, if said twice, is the name of a South Pacific island?
5. Is Lego an American, French, Danish or Dutch invention?
6. Where are most oranges grown — USA, South Africa or Brazil?
7. When might a tradesman use a bubble to determine whether a job has been done properly?
8. Is the patron saint of police officers St Thomas, St Michael or St Paul?
9. The Scottish Parliament building can be found in which Edinburgh road?
10. How does the Latin phrase 'non compos mentis' translate into English?
11. Which part of a car contains an inertia reel?
12. Do you have to pay vehicle licence duty on a tractor?
13. What were leeries in days gone by?
14. The name of which Glasgow district means 'place of the badger'?
15. Which washing machine manufacturer used the slogan 'the appliance of science'?
16. Rearrange GNOMES REQUEST TIRED IAN to discover a long-running radio programme.

ANSWERS

1 A speed detection camera, invented by Dutchman Maus Gatsonides, 2 Kessock, Friarton, Kincardine, Erskine, 3 On your head. They were antennae attached by springs to a hairband, 4 VW Bora & Bora Bora, 5 Danish, 6 Brazil, 7 When it's in a spirit level, 8 St Michael, 9 Holyrood Road, 10 Not of sound mind, 11 The seatbelt, 12 No, 13 Lamplighters who went around with a long pole to light gas street lamps, 14 Ibrox. From brock, an old word for badger, 15 Zanussi, 16 Gardeners Question Time.

GENERAL KNOWLEDGE

Facts are fun!

1. What gives brown sugar its colouring?
2. Which US state begins with a word meaning to join?
3. Michael Palin, Sean Bean, Prince Naseem Hamed and Joe Cocker were all born in which Yorkshire city?
4. Which Glasgow district contains the name of a precious stone?
5. Would you find a bonobo in a delicatessen, florist's shop, zoo or coffee shop?
6. In Lewis Carroll's *Alice In Wonderland*, what does the caterpillar smoke?
7. Pick the odd one out from these snooker players — John Higgins, Stephen Hendry, Ronnie O'Sullivan, Graeme Dott.
8. Providence is the capital of which US state?
9. What name is given to clock chimes that mimic Big Ben?
10. Is Melton Mowbray famous for its sponge cakes, pork pies or currant buns?
11. Would you find a pergola in a garage workshop, an optician's shop, a garden or a dentist's surgery?
12. It's generally believed that Judas Iscariot had what colour of hair?
13. In TV's *Only Fools And Horses* did the Trotters live in Streatham, Brixton, Lewisham or Peckham?
14. In Irish mythology what do leprechauns do for a living?
15. Which US state is known as the 'Volunteer' state?
16. How many toes do domestic cats have?

ANSWERS

1 Colouring either comes from the molasses in unrefined sugar or molasses added to the refined product, 2 Connecticut, 3 Sheffield, 4 Garnethill, 5 Zoo, it's a pygmy chimpanzee, 6 A hookah, a tobacco pipe where smoke is drawn through a pipe from a jar of water, 7 Ronnie O'Sullivan is the only Englishman, 8 Rhode Island, 9 Westminster Chimes, 10 Pork pies, 11 Garden, it's a structure for climbing plants, hanging baskets etc, 12 Red, 13 Peckham, 14 They're shoemakers, 15 Tennessee, 16 18. Five on each forepaw and four on each back paw.

The SUNDAY POST
FAMILY
QUIZ BOOK

BRAINBOX

For smarties only!

1. Approximately how much of the human body is made up of water — 25%, 45% or 65%?
2. Magnesium Sulphate has a more common name. What is it?
3. What do you get if you multiply volts by amps?
4. What can be igneus, sedimentary or metamorphic?
5. Its chemical name is acetylsalicylic acid. What is it more widely known as?
6. What is the difference between fog and mist?
7. Which has larger molecules — oil or water?
8. Are your carpal bones in your wrists or ankles?
9. What is the name given to the belt of low pressure over the Equator?
10. When milk goes sour, what kind of acid is formed?
11. The chemical symbol Sn signifies what?
12. In which year did the Space Shuttle first take off from Cape Canaveral?
13. What is the common name for Rubella?
14. Taxus is the botanical name for which evergreen tree or hedging plant?
15. What, in Fahrenheit, is normal body temperature?
16. If you suffer from mysophobia, do you fear death, dirt or the dark?

ANSWERS

1 65%, 2 Epsom Salts, 3 Watts, 4 Rock, 5 Aspirin, 6 If visibility is over 1100 yards, it is mist, but if it's under 1100 yards, it's fog, 7 Oil, 8 Lower hand and wrist, 9 The Doldrums, 10 Lactic Acid, 11 Tin, 12 April 1981, 13 German Measles, 14 The yew, 15 98.6, 16 Dirt.

GENERAL KNOWLEDGE

Quite quizzical!

● 1-5 Quite quiet! ● 6-11 Quite qualified! ● 12-16 Quite quick!

1. A windjammer would be most at home on an open hillside, on top of a tower, at sea or on a space satellite?
2. What is a loblolly — a chocolate cream dessert, a desert rat, a Chinese passenger trolley or a pine tree?
3. Comedian Charles Springall became famous after he changed his name to what?
4. How did the Red Sea get its name?
5. In the *Starsky & Hutch* TV series what were the first names of the two main characters?
6. What are the two most common reasons given for absence from work in the UK?
7. What makes hard water hard?
8. What kind of fish has another word for beer in its name?
9. Is your spleen located on the right or left side of your abdomen?
10. What kind of writing paper might remind you of a jester's hat?
11. How many yards are there in a mile?
12. Bo'ness in West Lothian is an abbreviation of what?
13. Can you see the initials VSOP on bottles of beer, vodka, wine or brandy?
14. What is Sarah Ferguson's middle name?
15. Complete the line from the nursery rhyme *Oranges and Lemons*, 'When I grow rich, say _____'.
16. Where were the 1996 Olympic Games held? Seoul, Atlanta, Barcelona or Montreal?

ANSWERS

1 At sea. It's a sailing ship, 2 A pine tree, 3 Charlie Drake, 4 Because the algae which grows in it makes the water appear red at certain times of year, 5 Dave Starsky and Ken Hutchinson, 6 Stress and lower back pain, 7 Calcium and magnesium, 8 An alewife, 9 The left, 10 Foolscap, 11 1760, 12 Borrowstounness, 13 Brandy — it stands for Very Special Old Pale, 14 Margaret, 15 The bells of Shoreditch, 16 Atlanta.

GENERAL KNOWLEDGE

How much do YOU know?

1. What were Kasparov, Karpov, Korchnoi and Kramnik famous for?
2. The Isle of Man's TT motor cycle races are world famous. What does TT stand for?
3. Mel C was a Spice Girl. Does the 'C' stand for Cunningham, Chisholm or Clark?
4. What's the proper job description for: a) a chippie, b) a sparkie, c) a brickie?
5. Why do boxers fight in a 'ring' when it's square?
6. On a standard button phone, where is the star key?
7. Why do we refer to an SOS as a Mayday?
8. Which TV series are or were filmed in the following Yorkshire villages: a) Holmfirth b) Goathland?
9. What is Prince William's full name?
10. Which is the most popular breed of pet dog in Britain?
11. In which month of the year was the 1997 General Election held?
12. In the Poldark novels, what was the name of Ross Poldark's home?
13. Queensland and Northern Territories in Australia gave their name to what national institution?
14. Why was Hollywood selected as the location for America's film industry?
15. Which type of headgear should remind you of: a) a Royal residence, b) Darren Gough, c) rasps?
16. Who were the female leads in the film *White Christmas*?

ANSWERS

1 Playing chess, 2 Tourist Trophy, 3 Chisholm, 4 a) Carpenter, b) electrician, c) bricklayer, 5 In the early days of prizefighting, bouts were held outside with spectators forming a 'ring' around the fighters, 6 Bottom left, 7 From 'M'aidez', French for 'help me', 8 a) Last Of The Summer Wine, b) Heartbeat, 9 William Arthur Philip Louis Windsor, 10 Labrador Retriever, 11 May, 12 Nampara, 13 Qantas, the Australian Airline, 14 California sunlight allowed movie making outdoors all year round, 15 a) Balmoral, b) bowler, (c) berets, 16 Rosemary Clooney and Vera Ellen.

The SUNDAY POST FAMILY QUIZ BOOK

SPORT
Actively awesome!

1. A face-off occurs in which sport?
2. The football team, Sampdoria, come from which country?
3. If a cricket umpire has his right arm straight out to the side, what is he indicating?
4. What is the second-highest score possible with three darts?
5. In which sport do the Green Bay Packers and the New England Patriots compete?
6. Matthew Hayden was top-scoring batsman in the 2007 cricket World Cup. What nationality is he?
7. Which country did Sir Vivian Richards represent in cricket?
8. Who was manager of Glasgow Rangers before Walter Smith took over for the second time?
9. How many Wimbledon Singles titles did Pete Sampras win? 7, 8 or 9?
10. True or false — skeet is a form of clay pigeon shooting?
11. If you were watching a football match between Getafe and Levante, which country would you be in?
12. In judo, what colour of belt do beginners wear?
13. What is the tennis 'Grand Slam'?
14. With which sport would you associate the term 'half-court-press'?
15. Which football team play their home matches at Fratton Park?
16. Which football team won the 2007 Champions League final in Athens?

ANSWERS

1 Ice Hockey, 2 Italy, 3 No-ball, 4 177, 5 American Football, 6 Australian, 7 West Indies, 8 Paul Le Guen, 9 Seven, 10 True, 11 Spain, 12 White, 13 Wimbledon, French Open, Australian Open and US Open, 14 Basketball, 15 Portsmouth FC, 16 AC Milan.

SPORT
Fit and healthy!

1. With which sport would you associate the Chester Jets and the DMU Leicester Riders?
2. In which year did boxing legend Mohammed Ali change his name from Cassius Clay?
3. How many feathers can be fixed to a badminton shuttlecock?
4. In which sport did Johnny Weissmuller, of *Tarzan* fame, excel?
5. Which sport is played at The Belfry? Cricket, archery, golf or horseracing?
6. What is a period of play in polo called?
7. Who was 'The Crafty Cockney'?
8. For which two Scottish clubs did Argentinian footballer Claudio Caniggia play?
9. In which town do Rugby Union side London Wasps play their home matches?
10. If you execute a camel-spin, which sport are you practicing? Gymnastics, skating or diving?
11. A 'wide receiver' is a position in which sport?
12. In which city is the Australian Open tennis championship held?
13. If you were faced with speed drives, loop drives and counter drives, which sport would you be playing?
14. What is the maximum circumference of a ten-pin bowling ball? 2.25 feet, 2.50 feet or 2.75 feet?
15. In which sport would you find the Centurions playing the Vikings?
16. With which county side did cricketer Michael Vaughan make his name?

ANSWERS

1 Basketball, 2 1964, 3 16, 4 Swimming, 5 Golf, 6 A chukka, 7 Darts player Eric Bristow, 8 Dundee and Rangers, 9 High Wycombe, 10 Ice skating, 11 American football, 12 Melbourne, 13 Table tennis, 14 2.25 feet, 15 Rugby League, 16 Yorkshire.

GENERAL KNOWLEDGE

It's a festive fizzer.

● 1-5 No cheer here! ● 6-11 Ring out the bells! ● 12-16 What a cracker!

1. If Wishee Washee is on stage, which Christmas pantomime are you watching?
2. Rearrange SOME TITLE to find something we hang up at Christmas.
3. Why was December 25 chosen as the date to celebrate Christmas?
4. What line follows 'Once in Royal David's City' in the popular carol?
5. Which monarch made the first Christmas Day broadcast to the nation?
6. Why do we wear paper hats at Christmas parties?
7. Was there really a King Wenceslas?
8. Why do we take our Christmas trees down on the 12th day?
9. In the Christmas song, how many pipers piping are there?
10. Why are Christmas hymns called carols?
11. 'Look to the future now it's only just begun' are lyrics from which Christmas pop song?
12. What are the last five words in the song *Rudolph The Red-Nosed Reindeer?*
13. The following people have names with a Christmas connection: a) *Deal or No Deal* presenter, b) *Countdown* girl, c) *The King And I* star.
14. Who or what is a 'tannenbaum'?
15. In which ocean is Christmas Island?
16. In which year during World War One was the unofficial 'Christmas truce' between British and German forces?

━━━━━ ANSWERS ━━━━━

1 Aladdin, 2 Mistletoe, 3 To detract from the winter solstice, which was a pagan festival, 4 Stood a lowly cattle shed, 5 King George V in 1932, 6 From a Roman custom where masters and slaves padded roles and wore mock crowns for fun, 7 Yes, 8 It was 12 days after Christ's birth that the Wise Men arrived at the stable, 9 Eleven, 10 Thought to be adapted from carole, an old word meaning 'round dance with singing', 11 Merry Xmas Ev'rybody by Slade, 12 You'll go down in history, 13 a) Noel Edmonds, b) Carol Vorderman, c) Yul) Brynner, 14 It's German for 'Christmas tree', 15 Indian, 16 1914.

The SUNDAY POST
FAMILY
QUIZ BOOK

GENERAL KNOWLEDGE

Quite quizzical!

1. Who in their profession would use Bordeaux Mixture — a wine merchant, a pharmacist, a gardener or a beauty therapist?
2. What is sick building syndrome?
3. What is a cummerbund?
4. Where is Edward VIII buried ?
5. What is a burgee on a yacht?
6. Rearrange TRIP A BREW PACKER to recall a No.1 Beatles hit.
7. *Pret-a-Porter* was a successful 1994 film. What is the English translation?
8. In what year did Michael Jackson and Lisa Marie Presley get married — 1990, 1992, 1994 or 1996?
9. Who wrote the *Tracy Beaker* stories?
10. What is the approximate distance between Earth and the sun — 33 million miles, 66 million miles, 93 million miles or 133 million miles?
11. Demetria Guynes found fame in the movie world when she changed her name to what?
12. Who was the first actor to be nominated for an Oscar posthumously — James Dean, Marilyn Monroe, River Phoenix or Humphrey Bogart?
13. Name three Shakespearean plays in which ghosts appear.
14. In The Bible where did Moses receive the Ten Commandments?
15. We've all heard of *Roget's Thesaurus*, but what nationality was Roget?
16. Why were British sailors nicknamed 'limeys'?

■■■■ ANSWERS ■■■■

1 A gardener, it's a lime and copper sulphate mixture, 2 Symptoms experienced by groups of people, thought to be caused by the building they work in, 3 A gentleman's waistband, 4 Frogmore, Windsor, 5 An identification flag, 6 Paperback Writer. 7 Ready to wear. 8 1994, 9 Jacqueline Wilson, 10 About 93 million miles, 11 Demi Moore, 12 James Dean, 13 Julius Caesar, Richard III, Hamlet or Macbeth, 14 Mount Sinai, 15 British, 16 Ships' crews were given limes to help combat scurvy.

KIDS' STUFF

Young at heart!

1. What was the name of the household pet in *The Flintstones*?
2. Who played the part of Elizabeth Swann in the *Pirates of the Caribbean* movies?
3. In which Italian city is the Bridge of Sighs?
4. What is a 'trousseau'?
5. Which famous king was reputed to have burnt the cakes?
6. What is the connection between Mordred, Galahad and Lancelot?
7. Who are Alex Turner, Jamie Cook, Matt Helder and Nick O'Malley better know as?
8. What organisation preceded the United Nations?
9. What are the surnames of the TV couple Richard and Judy?
10. What type of animal are the Appaloosa, Palomino and Hanoverian?
11. Who was the first person to reach the South Pole?
12. If you were travelling down the River Tiber, which major city would you pass through?
13. Who was the 'Lady with the Lamp'?
14. What, in Cockney rhyming slang, are 'apples and pears'?
15. Who was Boadicea?
16. Which city is further north, Glasgow or Edinburgh?

ANSWERS

1 Dino, 2 Keira Knightley, 3 Venice, 4 A bride's outfit, 5 Alfred, 6 They were all knights of King Arthur's Round Table, 7 Arctic Monkeys, 8 The League of Nations, 9 Richard Madeley and Judy Finnigan, 10 Horses, 11 Roald Amundsen, 12 Rome, 13 Florence Nightingale, 14 Stairs, 15 A tribal queen who waged war against the Romans in the First Century, 16 Edinburgh.

ENTERTAINMENT

Are you a star solver?

1. In the poem, which bird did the Ancient Mariner kill?
2. Who wrote the music for the famous musical *Oklahoma!*?
3. Who played King George in the film *The Madness Of King George*?
4. Was JM Barrie's *The Admirable Crichton* a butler, sea-captain or spy?
5. What film's central action was of a chariot race?
6. How many drones are there on a set of bagpipes — three, four or five?
7. Name the author of *Bravo Two Zero*.
8. Who got to the No.1 spot in 1970 with *Spirit In The Sky*?
9. In RL Stevenson's *Treasure Island* what was the name of the treasure-hunters' ship?
10. Who composed the *William Tell Overture*?
11. Who were the very first presenters of TV's *Blue Peter*?
12. The play *Blithe Spirit* was written by GB Shaw, Harold Pinter or Noel Coward?
13. In which country is the opera *Aida* set?
14. Who played the title role in the film *Dr Zhivago*?
15. Louis L'Amour was an American writer famous for writing what kind of novels?
16. Curly and Pieface are friends of which well-known comic character?

1 An albatross, 2 Richard Rogers, 3 Nigel Hawthorne, 4 Butler, 5 Ben Hur, 6 Three, 7 Andy McNab, 8 Norman Greenbaum, 9 The Hispaniola, 10 Rossini, 11 Christopher Trace and Leila Williams, 12 Noel Coward, 13 Egypt, 14 Omar Sharif, 15 Westerns, 16 Dennis the Menace.

GENERAL KNOWLEDGE

How much do YOU know?

1. The July Course and the Rowley Mile can be found on which English racecourse?
2. Which singing voice falls between baritone and alto?
3. Can you think of four alternative names for the devil?
4. What is the most common type of colour blindness?
5. We've all heard of the Aurora Borealis, The Northern Lights, but what is the proper name for the Southern Lights?
6. Name three members of the Tracy family from TV's *Thunderbirds*.
7. What is the smallest breed of dog?
8. Is a rebec something to spend or play?
9. Why is the watermark on banknotes so called?
10. Solve the following clues to TV chefs: a) Greek island, b) Dad was Chancellor, c) Moray Firth town.
11. If fruit is described as compote, how is it usually cooked?
12. How did the expression 'I haven't heard a dicky bird' originate?
13. What does Brava in Costa Brava mean?
14. Drop a letter from something that grows on trees to find part of a roof.
15. Do female robins have red breasts?
16. In which century did the Hundred Years War between France and England commence?

ANSWERS

1 Newmarket, 2 Tenor, 3 Satan, Beelzebub, Lucifer, Auld Nick etc, 4 The inability to distinguish between green and red, 5 Aurora Australis, 6 Any three from Scott, John, Virgil, Gordon, Alan, Jeff, 7 Chihuahua, 8 Play, it's a small violin-like instrument, 9 Because it's imprinted when the paper is still wet, 10 a) Gary Rhodes, b) Nigella Lawson, c) Nick Nairn, 11 It's stewed or cooked in a syrup, 12 It's rhyming slang, Dicky bird — word, 13 It means brave or wild, in reference to its rugged coastline, 14 Leaves to eaves, 15 Yes, 16 Fourteenth.

GENERAL KNOWLEDGE
Take the test.

1. Which famous Scottish monument sits at the top of Abbey Craig?
2. When were dog licences abolished?
3. What's the difference between orange juice and orange squash?
4. What five letter word provides a link between trapped, raw and ending?
5. How many records are guests on radio's *Desert Island Discs* asked to choose?
6. Pick the odd one out — burritos, quesadillas, bhajis and enchiladas.
7. Which Scottish Premier League football player is nicknamed 'Elvis'?
8. Do thunderstorms occur more frequently during warm or cold spells of weather?
9. What is thatch on a lawn?
10. If you are standing with your arms akimbo, what position have you adopted?
11. Why is a minister's house called a manse?
12. Name six British cheeses.
13. Which American bandleader was known as the 'King of Swing'?
14. Why do we advise people to take a tall story with 'a pinch of salt'?
15. What and where is the Skagerrak?
16. By what other name is the Battle of Aboukir Bay known: a) Battle of the Somme, b) Battle of Orleans, c) Battle of the Nile?

ANSWERS

1 The Wallace Monument, 2 1987, 3 Orange juice is squeezed from oranges, orange squash is concentrated and has other ingredients, 4 Nerve, 5 Eight, 6 Bhajis. They're an Indian food. The others are Mexican, 7 Steven Pressley, 8 Warm spells. They're caused by warm updrafts of air, 9 A build-up of dead grass, leaves, stems and roots, 10 Elbows bent, hands on hips, 11 From the Latin 'mansa', a dwelling, 12 Cheddar, Cheshire, Dunlop, Lancashire, Red Leicester, Stilton, Caerphilly etc, 13 Benny Goodman, 14 Because, like insipid food, salt makes it easier to swallow, 15 A stretch of water between Denmark and Norway, 16 Battle of the Nile.

KIDS' STUFF

Young at heart!

● 1-5 Year one! ● 6-11 Year four! ● 12-16 Year seven!

1. Richmal Crompton wrote which series of childrens' novels?
2. Who or what was *Skippy* in the TV series of the same name?
3. Unscramble A TACK TART to find a 'creative' TV show.
4. Name the four female members of *The Broons*.
5. Which *Pirates of the Caribbean* star has the middle names Jonathan Blanchard?
6. Who or what were teddy bears named after?
7. What is the name of the fun-park just outside Motherwell?
8. Where would you find Avalanche, Valhalla and Wild Mouse?
9. With which instrument do you associate Yehudi Menuhin?
10. How are Amelle, Heidi and Keisha better known?
11. Which mythological king had the 'golden touch'?
12. In which Scottish city is the Burrell Collection?
13. How are Bill and Ben better known?
14. Which is higher, the Tower of Big Ben or the London Eye?
15. In which county would you find Lake Windermere?
16. In the rhyme *Oranges and Lemons*, what did the Bells of St Martins sing?

ANSWERS

1 *Just William*, 2 A kangaroo, 3 Art Attack, 4 Maw, Maggie, Daphne and the Bairn, 5 Orlando Bloom, 6 US President Theodore Roosevelt, 7 M and D's, 8 At Blackpool Pleasure Beach. They are all amusement rides, 9 Violin, 10 Sugababes, 11 Midas, 12 Glasgow, 13 The Flowerpot Men, 14 London Eye at 135 metres. Big Ben is 96.3 metres, 15 Cumbria, 16 You owe me five farthings.

GENERAL KNOWLEDGE

Facts are fun!

1. Which Rolf Harris song was the last No.1 of the 1960s?
2. What are you interested in if you're consulting a copy of *Glass's Guide*?
3. On the ground a group of geese is a gaggle, but what are they known as in flight?
4. The following clues are for words or phrases ending in 'aire':
   a) soldier, b) rich man, c) survey.
5. Is a marimba a poisonous snake, musical instrument or African tribal dance?
6. Which motorcycle manufacturer produced the Bonneville?
7. Which German word, commonly used in English, means 'noisy ghost'?
8. Why do we call meat and pastry pasties 'bridies'?
9. Which one of the following isn't a dance? Glitterati, cakewalk or lindy hop?
10. Which grow larger — rhododendrons or azaleas?
11. What is the largest inland sea in the world?
12. The story of Noah's Ark is told in which book of the Old Testament?
13. Which lifeline is usually the first choice for contestants on *Who Wants To Be A Millionaire*? — ask the audience, phone a friend or 50/50?
14. In the rhyme, who saw Cock Robin die?
15. Who wrote *The Canterbury Tales*?
16. Who was known as the 'Iron Chancellor'?

ANSWERS

1 *Two Little Boys*, 2 Motor vehicles. It's a used vehicle price guide, 3 A skein, 4 a) legionnaire, b) millionaire, c) questionnaire, 5 It's a musical instrument, 6 Triumph, 7 Poltergeist, 8 Possibly derived from bride's pie, a recipe once popular at weddings, 9 Glitterati — a name for a group of wealthy or famous people, 10 Rhododendrons generally, 11 Caspian Sea, 12 Genesis, 13 Ask the audience, 14 The fly with his little eye, 15 Geoffrey Chaucer, 16 Bismarck.

ENTERTAINMENT

Test your celebrity rating.

● 1-5 Switched off! ● 6-11 Switched on! ● 12-16 Star quality!

1. Who was the author of *Ivanhoe*?
2. Who recorded *Oh, Carol!* in 1959?
3. Who played Moses in the 1956 film, *The Ten Commandments*?
4. How many squares can a rook move forward, in chess?
5. Who had a hit in 1980 with *De Do Do Do, De Da Da Da*?
6. Manor Farm is the setting for which classic book?
7. Who starred in the classic TV drama series, *Kavanagh Q.C.*?
8. Apart from writing poetry, what government job did Robert Burns have?
9. In which TV series did Frank Windsor and Stratford Johns first appear as policemen?
10. When was musician/singer Stevie Wonder born — 1948, 1949 or 1950?
11. Who played the malfunctioning cowboy robot in the 1973 movie, *Westworld*?
12. Captain Ahab was the skipper in which famous novel?
13. In which year did Elvis Presley have a No.1 hit with *Jailhouse Rock*?
14. Name the actor who played Siegfried Farnon in TV's *All Creatures Great And Small*.
15. True or false — Arthur Conan Doyle was a doctor by profession?
16. 'Reader, I married him' is a line from which classic book?

■ ANSWERS ■

GENERAL KNOWLEDGE

Quite quizzical!

1. Was Thomas Jefferson the second, third or fourth President of the USA?
2. Where can you find Beecher's Brook?
3. How did the expression 'no room to swing a cat' originate?
4. What was the top-selling film soundtrack album of the 1970s — *Grease, Saturday Night Fever,* or *The Rocky Horror Picture Show*?
5. According to the song who was 'Born on a mountain top in Tennessee'?
6. Is a heptaglot a poem of seven verses, a plant with seven leaves or a book in seven languages?
7. Which pop star played the scarecrow in the 1978 movie *The Wiz*?
8. Why is someone's double called a doppelganger?
9. Which famous Liverpudlian published a book of poetry called *Blackbird Singing*?
10. Which is the longest Shakespeare play?
11. Where in the body are your pectoral muscles?
12. Someone who is talking nonsense can be said to be talking baloney, but what is baloney?
13. Which eight-letter word can precede gown, room and table?
14. Who was author Johanna Spyri's orphaned heroine?
15. Which British monarch was born in The Hague?
16. In which Australian state is the town of Alice Springs?

ANSWERS

1 Third, 2 At Aintree racecourse. It's a well-known hurdle, 3 From the cat o' nine tails, a long whip once used as punishment on sailing ships. It was administered on deck as there was no room below, 4 Saturday Night Fever, 5 Davy Crockett, 6 A book in seven languages, 7 Michael Jackson, 8 It comes from the German meaning double walker or double goer, 9 Sir Paul McCartney, 10 Hamlet, 11 In your chest, 12 A type of sausage, from the Italian town of Bologna, 13 Dressing, 14 Heidi, 15 William III, 16 Northern Territory.

BRAINBOX

For smarties only!

1. Who is connected with the following ships — *Adventure, Discovery, Endeavour, Resolution*?
2. What does a 'blood count' mean, in medical terms?
3. In a sailing boat, what are the sheets?
4. Sodium Bicarbonate, Sodium Borate, Sodium Chloride — which is more commonly known as household salt?
5. What is Dutch metal?
6. Is your occipital artery behind your knee, behind your ear or under your arm?
7. Is periwinkle a trailing plant, a light blue colour or an edible gasteropod?
8. If you drove from Glasgow to London, approximately how many miles would you travel?
9. What would you see if you visited Lascaux Caves in France?
10. Grapes contain which kind of acid?
11. Does a craniometer measure the density of milk, atmospheric pressure or the size of your skull?
12. Michael Collins was the third man to set foot on the moon — true or false?
13. Which part of an egg is the albumen — the yolk or the white?
14. If a bird is described as 'conirostral', does it have — a dark red breast, wide webbed feet or a cone-shaped beak?
15. Does a refractor telescope use lenses or mirrors?
16. What name is given to a railway which uses cables to move the carriages?

ANSWERS

1 Captain Cook, 2 It determines the number of red or white blood cells in a known volume of blood, 3 The ropes controlling the angle of the sails to the wind, 4 Sodium Chloride, 5 An alloy of copper and zinc, 6 Behind your ear, 7 It can be all three, 8 Around 405 miles, 9 Preserved examples of art by prehistoric man, 10 Tartaric acid, 11 The size of your skull, 12 False — he stayed in the Command Module of Apollo XI, orbiting the moon, 13 The white, 14 A cone-shaped beak, 15 Lenses, 16 Funicular.

SPORT
Actively awesome!

● 1-5 Relegation! ● 6-11 Mid-table! ● 12-16 Champions!

1. Scot David Wilkie won Olympic gold in 1976. What for?
2. What is it called if you knock down all ten pins with one bowl in a game of tenpin bowling?
3. Who won Wimbledon Women's Singles Championship in 1984? Chris Evert or Martina Navratilova?
4. How long is an ice hockey rink?
5. What do Keke Rosberg and Mika Hakkinen have in common?
6. True or false — The inside of a cricket ball is made of leather?
7. Who defeated Dundee United in the semi-finals of the 1984 European Cup?
8. What was the title of the England World Cup Squad's No.1 hit of 1970?
9. How many innings are there in a professional game of American baseball — seven, nine or eleven?
10. With which sport would you associate Jonah Barrington?
11. Which county cricket club has its headquarters at Old Trafford?
12. Stamford Bridge is the home of which English football team?
13. Which is not an Olympic running distance? 100 metres, 400 metres or 600 metres?
14. Who are the Springboks?
15. Name the first British football team to win the European Cup.
16. Roughly how long is the course of the Oxford/Cambridge Boat Race — over three, four or five miles?

ANSWERS

1 200 metres breaststroke, 2 A strike, 3 Martina Navratilova, 4 200 feet (61 metres), 5 They are Finns who have both won the World Motor Racing Championship, 6 False — it's made of cork, 7 AS Roma, 8 Back Home, 9 Nine, 10 Squash, 11 Lancashire, 12 Chelsea, 13 600 metres, 14 The South African national Rugby Union team, 15 Celtic, 16 Over four miles.

ENTERTAINMENT

Are you a star solver?

1. Is Roger the Dodger in the *Beano* or the *Dandy*?
2. In the film world, who were Benjamin Braddock and Mrs Robinson?
3. Did Wagner, the composer, die in 1881, 1882 or 1883?
4. Can you name each of *The Famous Five* from the Enid Blyton books?
5. From where in London did the BBC transmit its first TV service?
6. Complete the old Elton John song *Don't Shoot Me, I'm _____*.
7. Who wrote the novel, *The War of the Worlds*?
8. Scooby Doo is a cartoon cat, rabbit or dog?
9. What was the name of the camp host and entertainments manager in the classic TV sitcom, *Hi-de-Hi!*?
10. The Quarrymen found fame and fortune after changing their name to what?
11. Who co-starred with Laurence Olivier in the 1933 film *A Perfect Understanding*?
12. In Robert Louis Stevenson's novel, what are the first names of *Dr Jekyll and Mr Hyde*?
13. Who was the original presenter of the classic TV game show *The Golden Shot*?
14. What instrument did Charlie Parker, the jazz musician, play?
15. Who wrote the lyrics for Bernstein's *West Side Story*?
16. What is the name of the only Shakespeare play with an animal in the title?

ANSWERS

1 *The Beano*, 2 The leading characters in the film, *The Graduate*, 3 1883, 4 Julian, Dick, George, Anne and Timmy the dog, 5 Alexandra Palace, 6 Only The Piano Player, 7 HG Wells, 8 Dog, 9 Ted Bovis, 10 The Beatles, 11 Gloria Swanson, 12 Henry Jekyll, Edward Hyde, 13 Bob Monkhouse, 14 Saxophone, 15 Stephen Sondheim, 16 The Taming Of The Shrew.

ENTERTAINMENT

Test your celebrity rating.

1. Blanche Du Bois is a character in which famous play and film?
2. What nationality was the poet Ezra Pound — American, Irish or Welsh?
3. Name the two main stars of the classic police TV programme *The Sweeney*?
4. Who composed the music for the ballet *Sleeping Beauty*?
5. Which member of The Who played the title role in the 1975 Ken Russell film *Tommy*?
6. What was the colour of the Brick Road followed by Dorothy in *The Wizard Of Oz*?
7. *Tubular Bells* by Mike Oldfield was used in which horror film?
8. Which leading actor made his name on the TV comedy series *Mork and Mindy*?
9. Ding-Ding-Ding, A Bi Ni Bi, Boom-Bang-A-Bang and Diggi-Loo Diggi-Ley. What's the connection?
10. His films include *Batman Returns, Romancing The Stone* and Twins. Name the actor.
11. Which fictional Bear is the oldest — Pooh, Biffo or Rupert?
12. *King Of The Road* was a No.1 hit in 1965, for whom?
13. What does 'sotto voce' mean?
14. 'May the Force be with you!' is a well-used phrase from which film of the Seventies?
15. Which book features the land of Brobdingnag?
16. Can you name two bands of which Scottish singer Annie Lennox was a member?

ANSWERS

1 *A Streetcar Named Desire*, 2 *American*, 3 *John Thaw and Dennis Waterman*, 4 *Tchaikovsky*, 5 *Roger Daltrey*, 6 *Yellow*, 7 *The Exorcist*, 8 *Robin Williams*, 9 *They have all been winning songs in The Eurovision Song Contest*, 10 *Danny DeVito*, 11 *Rupert (1920), Pooh (1926), Biffo (1948)*, 12 *Roger Miller*, 13 *Whispered or scarcely audible*, 14 *Star Wars*, 15 *Gulliver's Travels*, 16 *Tourists, Eurythmics*.

GENERAL KNOWLEDGE

How much do YOU know?

1. How old was Michael Jackson when he had his first UK No.1 solo hit?
2. When did Edinburgh Zoo open —1913, 1926, 1930 or 1933?
3. If you suffered from triskaidekaphobia which number are you afraid of? 6, 666, 13 or 33?
4. Unscramble A RAG MAN to discover this kind of word?
5. Chicago lies on the bank of which of the Great Lakes?
6. Can you think of a place in Ayrshire that sounds like something people dance around?
7. What was the name of Walt Disney's first full-length cartoon film?
8. George Orwell wrote his novel *1984* on which Scottish island — Islay, Jura, Eigg or Arran?
9. What is a dwarf pygmy goby?
10. An American hotel and a Roman emperor both gave their names to something we eat. What is it?
11. Does cinnamon come from the roots, the leaves, the bark or the seeds of the tree?
12. Which vegetable is also a European nationality?
13. Elaine Bickerstaff found fame in showbusiness after changing her name to what?
14. What causes the sensation of pins and needles in your arm or leg?
15. With which TV programme would you associate Paul Merton and Ian Hislop?
16. In which US state is Mount McKinley?

ANSWERS

1 22. He first hit the top spot with One Day In Your Life in May 1981, 2 1913, 3 Number 13, 4 Anagram, 5 Lake Michigan, 6 Maybole, like 'maypole', 7 Snow White and The Seven Dwarfs, released in 1937, 8 Jura, 9 A small species of fish, 10 Salad. Waldorf salad and Caesar salad, 11 The inner bark, 12 Swede, 13 Elaine Paige, 14 The feeling is caused by a disturbance in the blood flow and movement of nerve impulses by pressure on your limbs, 15 Have I Got News For You, 16 Alaska.

GENERAL KNOWLEDGE

Take the test.

● 1-5 Must try harder! ● 6-11 Could do better! ● 12-16 Top of the class!

1. How many gallons were in the old measure known as a bushel?
2. Pentland Crown is a type of sheep, paint or potato?
3. Can you list the contents of a Pina Colada?
4. What does ICBM stand for?
5. Which European make of car has a lion as its badge?
6. What name is given to a temporary bridge of steel girders?
7. On The Isle of Man, what is the Tynwald?
8. Chianti is a wine from which area of Italy?
9. How much was a bawbee worth?
10. In what year was everyone over the age of 21 given the right to vote in Britain?
11. Was Sir Laurence Van Der Post a novelist, conductor or poet?
12. What is the minimum age that an American citizen can become president?
13. Lee-Enfield, Springfield, Winchester, are all types of what?
14. When were 'L' plates first introduced for learner drivers in Britain? 1933, 1934 or 1935?
15. In which South American country is the language known as Guarani spoken?
16. Name a sea creature which sticks to ships.

ANSWERS

1 Eight gallons, 2 Potato, 3 Pineapple juice, coconut cream, white rum, 4 Inter-Continental Ballistic Missile, 5 Peugeot, 6 A Bailey Bridge, 7 The governing assembly, 8 Tuscany, 9 A half penny in pre-decimal coinage, 10 1928, 11 Novelist, 12 35, 13 Rifle, 14 1935, 15 Paraguay, 16 Barnacle or limpet.

GENERAL KNOWLEDGE

Take the test.

● 1-5 Must try harder! ● 6-11 Could do better! ● 12-16 Top of the class!

1. What are 'invisible exports'?
2. What does ESP mean?
3. When tightening a screw, do you turn it clockwise or anti-clockwise?
4. Where did Stan Laurel, Dennis The Menace and the Mona Lisa all appear together?
5. In heraldry, what are 'attires' — stag's antlers or suits of armour?
6. How many squares are there in a game of noughts and crosses?
7. Cobol, Fortran, Java are all what?
8. What is the main colour of the Royal Stewart tartan — red, blue or green?
9. What is kapok?
10. Is the Tropic of Cancer north or south of the Equator?
11. How many sheets of paper were in a quire?
12. What are the two main components of cement?
13. What is, or was, a chandler?
14. The Americans call it a zip code — what is it in Britain?
15. If you have an LLB degree, what is your area of expertise?
16. Pewter is an alloy of which two metals?

ANSWERS

GENERAL KNOWLEDGE

How much do YOU know?

1. Where is the Sea of Storms?
2. How many seconds are there in seven hours?
3. What is Nelson's statue in Trafalgar Square made from?
4. Is the Baleno a model of car from Volvo, Suzuki or VW?
5. Who might use a dibber?
6. Epaulettes, tabard and espallieres would all be found on what?
7. In which London Park would you find the Serpentine Lake and Rotten Row?
8. What is unusual about the brakes on speedway racing motorcycles?
9. Which car manufacturer produces the Focus?
10. Give the legal term used to describe a written voluntary statement, given under oath.
11. Describe the heraldic term 'fess'.
12. Is Stromboli — a type of violin, a well-matured Italian cheese, or an active volcano?
13. If you were sitting an exam described as 'viva voce', what does this mean?
14. For what is the company Dorling Kindersley famous?
15. If someone offered you an Abernethy, what kind of food would you receive?
16. Does 'demitasse' mean a type of barometer or a small coffee cup?

ANSWERS

1 On the moon, 2 25,200, 3 The body is stone, the head is metal, 4 Suzuki, 5 Gardener — it's a tool for making small holes, 6 A suit of armour, 7 Hyde Park, 8 There are no brakes on speedway motorcycles, 9 Ford, 10 An affidavit, 11 It's a wide horizontal stripe across a shield, 12 An active volcano on one of the Eolian islands, 13 It's an oral exam, 14 Educational books and cd roms, 15 A biscuit, 16 A small coffee cup.

GENERAL KNOWLEDGE

Take the test.

1. You can sail in one or you can drink from one. Which word fits both descriptions?
2. Saggitarius, the star sign, comes between Capricorn and Virgo — true or false?
3. The bird depicted on the old coin called a farthing was a robin, starling or wren?
4. Mullet, mussel, squid, oyster, which is the odd one out?
5. How many gallons in a magnum of Champagne?
6. Hemmorage, haemorrhage, haemmorrage — which is the correct spelling?
7. What is the RNLI?
8. Why would you carry a portmanteau?
9. Plane, chisel, pliers, saw — which is the odd one out?
10. Is henbane a breed of fowl, a poisonous plant or a disease?
11. In which branch of commerce does an actuary work?
12. Where would you find caulking?
13. What was the original name given to the statue now known as Eros at Piccadilly Circus in London?
14. Would you sit on, play with or drink kummel?
15. Can you name the title in UK peerage which comes between earl and baron?
16. What is telemetry?

ANSWERS

1 Schooner, 2 False — it's between Scorpio and Capricorn, 3 Wren, 4 Mullet — it is a fish with a backbone. The others are invertebrates, 5 Half a gallon, 6 Haemorrhage, 7 The Royal National Lifeboat Institution, 8 To put your clothes in — it's a suitcase, 9 Pliers - the other tools are for use with wood, 10 A poisonous plant, 11 Insurance, 12 On a boat — it's a kind of waterproofing glue, 13 The Shaftesbury Memorial, 14 Drink it, it's a liqueur, 15 Viscount, 16 Measurement at distance, such as when using instruments on board a satellite in space.

THE SUNDAY POST
FAMILY
QUIZ BOOK

SPORT

Actively awesome!

1. Is the 1500m track race classed as being long distance, middle distance or short distance?
2. The toe board at the front of a shot put circle is approximately how high?
3. How many Olympic medals did athlete Sebastian Coe win in his career?
4. The IIHF is the governing body for what chilly sport?
5. Name TV presenter Gabby Logan's ex-footballing father.
6. Which two top Italian football teams play in Turin?
7. In horse racing, when is a filly considered to be a mare?
8. Who was manager of Manchester United immediately before Alex Ferguson?
9. Which three disciplines make up a triathlon?
10. Who was the young South African girl who, briefly, ran bare-footed for Britain?
11. When was tennis reintroduced as an Olympic sport — 1980, 1984, 1988 or 1992?
12. Who captained the Italian World Cup winning team of 2006?
13. Which mainly female sport was pioneered by an American physical education instructor called Clara Gregory Baer in 1895?
14. With which exciting sport would you associate the name of Valentino Rossi?
15. Which world famous three-day event, a highlight of the equestrian calendar, is hosted by the Duke of Beaufort?
16. How many are in a standard tug of war team?

ANSWERS

1 Middle distance, 2 10cm (4"), 3 Four. Two gold and two silver, 4 Ice Hockey, 5 Terry Yorath, 6 Juventus and Turino, 7 At five years old, 8 Ron Atkinson, 9 Swimming, cycling and running, 10 Zola Budd, 11 1988, 12 Fabio Cannavaro, 13 Netball, 14 Motorcycle racing, especially MotoGP, 15 Badminton, 16 Eight.

GENERAL KNOWLEDGE

Quite quizzical!

1. The original colour of British pillar boxes was green — true or false?
2. What kind of creature is a godwit?
3. What was the name of the electric car invented by Sir Clive Sinclair?
4. If you are described as monogamous, how many people are you married to?
5. Who would use a pipette — a bagpipe player, a cake-maker or a scientist?
6. If you find a stamp with 'Sverige' on it, which country does it come from?
7. What is meant by the distaff side of the family?
8. What does AD stand for in, for example, 2005 AD?
9. Would you eat wrack?
10. Cherokee, Chipmunk, Comanche are all types of what?
11. To a zoologist, what is a monotreme?
12. Is an abalone — a rocky outcrop, a species of shellfish, or a small basket?
13. Who or what gave their name to the first month of the year?
14. What was made by pressing a mix of linseed oil, gum and ground cork onto coarse canvas?
15. Who might use an adze? A carpenter, an airline pilot or a circus acrobat?
16. The Star of Africa is — a large diamond, a locomotive, or a nickname for Bob Geldof?

ANSWERS

1 True, 2 A Wading bird, 3 The C5, 4 One, 5 A scientist, 6 Sweden, 7 The female line, 8 Anno Domini — Latin for 'in the year of our Lord', 9 Perhaps — it's an edible seaweed, 10 Light aircraft, 11 An egg-laying mammal, 12 A species of shellfish, 13 Janus, the two-headed Roman god, 14 Linoleum, 15 A carpenter, 16 A large diamond.

GENERAL KNOWLEDGE

Facts are fun!

1. What is meant by the Civil List?
2. Is zebu — the twelfth letter of the Greek alphabet, a type of humped ox or the monetary unit of Rwanda?
3. A three-towered castle is the assay mark or hallmark for which city, on gold or silver?
4. If you were given a champignon, would you: a) eat it, b) wear it, c) hang it on the wall?
5. What can be lengthened by being cut at both ends?
6. Normally, how many facets are there on a diamond — 58, 64 or 72?
7. Horse, sheep, badger, monkey — which is not a character on the Chinese calendar?
8. If a pavement is tessellated, what does this mean?
9. What rank is held by an Army officer with three 'pips', or stars, on his shoulder?
10. Whereabouts in a house might you find a jamb?
11. Lazy Daisy, Outline, Blanket and Buttonhole are all flowers — true or false?
12. A magnum of champagne is the equivalent of two, four or six bottles?
13. If someone sent you a double elephant, what would you do with it?
14. What cost America $7,200,000 in 1867?
15. If an old book is described as 'foxed' what does this mean?
16. In Cockney rhyming slang, where would you wear 'daisy roots'?

ANSWERS

1 The annuity payable to the Sovereign to maintain the royal household, 2 A type of humped ox, 3 Edinburgh, 4 a) Eat it — it's a mushroom, 5 A ditch, 6 58, 7 Badger, 8 It is made from flat pieces of stone in various colours arranged in a pattern, 9 Captain, 10 It's the side post of a doorway or window, 11 False, they are all embroidery stitches, 12 Two bottles, 13 Write on it, it's an old measure of paper, 14 The area of land now known as Alaska, 15 The pages are discoloured by brownish spots, 16 On your feet — they're boots.

GENERAL KNOWLEDGE

Take the test.

1. There are only three in Scotland — in Dumfries, Edinburgh and Kirriemuir. What are they?
2. Nevada, Iowa, Oregon, Utah. Only one of these US states has a coastline, but which one?
3. Where might you speak the language known as Sinhalese?
4. Which two seas are linked by the Suez Canal?
5. What is the maximum number of dots used to portray a single letter in Braille?
6. If your collar size is 15½ in Britain, what is it in France?
7. If you were given a smorrebrod in Denmark, what would you do with it?
8. What did the members of the Women's Institute of Rylstone do in 1999 to raise money for charity?
9. When tiling a floor, where should the first tile be laid?
10. Is Iceberg a type of apple?
11. What is the naval rank between Able Seaman and Petty Officer?
12. True or false — dalmatic is woven silk or linen with designs shown up by reflection of light?
13. In the game of Charades, how do you indicate that the subject is the name of something?
14. Which item of clothing was banned by law in 1746?
15. In what year did Sweden change from driving on the left to driving on the right?
16. Which is the only Zodiac sign not represented by a living creature?

ANSWERS

1 Camera Obscura, 2 Oregon, 3 Sri Lanka, 4 The Mediterranean and the Red Sea, 5 Six, 6 39, 7 Eat it — it's an open sandwich, 8 Posed nude for a calendar, 9 In the centre of a room. The centre point should be marked with a cross, and the tile corner placed on that point, 10 No — it's a type of lettuce, 11 Leading Seaman, 12 False — it's a bishop's vestment, 13 You pat your head, 14 The kilt, 15 1967, 16 Libra, the scales.

ENTERTAINMENT
Test your celebrity rating.

1. Which group backed Smokey Robinson in the late 1960s and early 1970s?
2. Malvolio appears in which Shakespeare play?
3. In the James Bond film *Goldfinger*, what was the name of the assassin with the deadly bowler hat?
4. How many white squares are there on a chess board?
5. What was Dorothy's dog called in *The Wizard Of Oz*?
6. *The Boxer, I Am A Rock* and *Homeward Bound* — who had hit singles with these songs?
7. In what classic novel would you find a house called Manderley?
8. The Usher Hall is a major performing venue in which city — Glasgow, Edinburgh or Stirling?
9. His books include *The Odessa File* and *The Dogs Of War*. Name the author.
10. In music, what is a bagatelle?
11. In what film and TV series would you have seen Hotlips Houlihan?
12. Who was born on 8th January 1935 at Tupelo, Mississippi, one of twin sons?
13. When did actor David Niven die — 1973, 1978 or 1983?
14. Lisa Minelli played a character called Sally Bowles in what film?
15. In *The Diary Of Anne Frank*, where did the heroine live?
16. Lena Martell topped the music charts in 1979 with which song?

ANSWERS

ENTERTAINMENT

Are you a star solver?

● 1-5 Star gazing! ● 6-11 Star bright! ● 12-16 Starring role!

1. What was author of *Three Men In A Boat*, Jerome K Jerome's middle name?
2. Was it Cat Stevens, Shakin' Stevens or Ray Stevens who had a hit in 1972 with *Morning Has Broken*?
3. Where does the *Dandy* comic's *Desperate Dan* live?
4. Who played *Ally McBeal* in the TV series of the same name?
5. Name the only single by Jimi Hendrix to reach the No.1 spot.
6. Fizz, Bella, Jake and _____ ? Who is missing?
7. If a musical piece is 'staccato' what does this mean?
8. In the nursery rhyme, where would you find *Little Polly Flinders*?
9. What did TS stand for, in the name of the poet TS Eliot?
10. Name the spaceship in Stanley Kubrik's classic film, *2001 — A Space Odyssey*?
11. Who refused *Oliver Twist* a second helping?
12. What was the title of the first James Bond film?
13. Who wrote the novel *Robinson Crusoe*?
14. What is the tenor Pavarotti's first name?
15. Who played TV's *Rumpole Of The Bailey*?
16. *Never Do A Tango With An Eskimo* was a hit for Alma Cogan in what year — 1953, 1954 or 1955?

THE SUNDAY POST
FAMILY QUIZ BOOK

GENERAL KNOWLEDGE

Quick Choice Quiz

1. Is a parang a gargoyle on the edge of a balcony, a poisonous insect or a Malayan knife?
2. Does pediment mean an early bicycle, a speech defect or an architectural feature?
3. How many square metres are there in a hectare? 100, 1,000 or 10,000?
4. In Morse Code, the letter represented by dot-dash-dot is R, T or V?
5. Chabichou is: a) a French cheese, b) a small deer, c) a Russian doll?
6. Is a grouper a complainer, a kind of fish or a large, two-handled basket?
7. If a doctor describes you as consumptive, which body part is affected — heart, lungs or liver?
8. Zampogna means a type of cheese, a musical instrument or a cactus?
9. How would you address a Cardinal — Your Grace, Your Holiness or Your Eminence?
10. Dead Men's Fingers is a card game, a complicated knot or a type of coral?
11. How many wheels did the horse-drawn carriage known as a landau have — two, four or six?
12. What are Eastern, Central, Mountain and Pacific?
13. Is the collective name for pigs — a pack, flock or drove?
14. Was Sir John Everett Millais a poet, an artist or a composer?
15. Is okra a giraffe-like animal, a gauze-like material or a tropical plant?
16. Was a tilbury an old-fashioned hat, an open two-wheeled carriage, or an oil lamp?

■ ANSWERS ■

1 A Malayan sheath-knife, 2 An architectural feature crowning the front of a building, 3 10,000, 4 R, 5 French cheese, 6 A kind of fish, 7 The lungs, 8 A musical instrument (a kind of bagpipes), 9 Your Eminence, 10 A type of coral, 11 Four, 12 Time zones in the USA, 13 Drove, 14 An artist, 15 Tropical plant, 16 An open two-wheeled carriage.

GENERAL KNOWLEDGE

How much do YOU know?

1. Muslin, velour, sorrel, brocade — which is the odd one out?
2. In Egyptian mythology, Anubis was the god of what?
3. When was Third Class abolished on the British railway system?
4. During the First World War what would you do with a Sopwith Camel?
5. The old Imperial measurement, one hundredweight, was roughly equal to how many kilogrammes?
6. What were Cora, Beatrice, Ruth, Beryl and Claymore?
7. What is the approximate weight of the bell known as Great Paul, in St Paul's Cathedral — almost 16, 17 or 18 tonnes?
8. Is lapis lazuli anything to do with rabbits?
9. True or false — a clinometer measures the size of your skull?
10. Does haemorrhage mean blood transfusion, clotted blood or loss of blood?
11. Where would you find a proscenium?
12. What can be a jewelled clasp on a coat, another name for a walrus and an international signalling code?
13. If a vegetable is described as legume, what does this actually mean?
14. George Thomas, Bernard Weatherill, Betty Boothroyd. What's the connection between the three politicians?
15. A mercer was involved in which trade: a) boot-making, b) silversmithing, c) candle-making, d) textile dealing?
16. The Red Arrows are a famous acrobatics team — true or false?

ANSWERS

1 Sorrel — it's a herb. The others are types of material, 2 Death, 3 1956, 4 Fly in it — it's an aeroplane, 5 Fifty, 6 North Sea Oilfields, 7 Almost 17 tonnes, 8 No — it's a semi-precious stone, 9 False. It is used in the building trade to measure angles of elevation, 10 Loss of blood, 11 In a theatre — it's the part of the stage in front of the curtain, 12 Morse, 13 It's a podded vegetable, like peas, 14 They have all held the position of Speaker of the House of Commons, 15 Textile dealing, 16 False. They're an aerobatics team.

ENTERTAINMENT

Test your celebrity rating.

1. Who is the star of TV's *A Touch Of Frost*?
2. What was singer Asa Yoelson's stage name?
3. In what year did Dawn have a hit with *Tie A Yellow Ribbon Round The Old Oak Tree*?
4. Sancho Panza was the squire to which story-book Spanish knight?
5. Who played the leading role in the TV series *Lovejoy*?
6. Dustin Hoffman won an Oscar for his performance in the film Rain Man, but in what year?
7. *Pretty Little Angel Eyes* and *Under The Moon Of Love* were two of this band's hits. Name the band.
8. Serjeant Buzfuz, Clara Cluck, Uriah Heep, Anastasia Rugg. Which one is not a Dickens character?
9. Who played *Rooster Cogburn* in the film of that name?
10. Was science-fiction writer Isaac Asimov born in America, Russia or Britain?
11. Strings, Brass, Percussion — what is the fourth section of the orchestra?
12. In the Australian song *Waltzing Matilda*, what is an Australian bushman's 'Matilda'?
13. Ruth Rendell created which detective?
14. Virgil Tibbs was the name of a plain-clothes policeman in which classic book and fim?
15. The playwright, Ibsen, was what nationality — Swedish, Dutch or Norwegian?
16. Phil Collins had his first hit records playing drums with which famous band?

ANSWERS

1 David Jason, 2 Al Jolson, 3 1973, 4 Don Quixote, 5 Ian McShane, 6 1988, 7 Showaddywaddy, 8 Clara Cluck, 9 John Wayne, 10 Russia, 11 Woodwind, 12 His pack, or swag, 13 Inspector Wexford, 14 In The Heat Of The Night, 15 Norwegian, 16 Genesis.

THE SUNDAY POST

FAMILY

QUIZ BOOK

KIDS' STUFF
Practically playtime!

1. What is the capital city of France?
2. According to the nursery rhyme, what did Jack Sprat eat?
3. In the books and films, who are Harry Potter's two best friends?
4. Which is the odd one out: a) Plug, b) Smiffy, c) Dennis, d) Wilfrid.
5. Can Albert Square be found in *Coronation Street, Emmerdale* or *EastEnders*?
6. What is special about the title character in the film *Babe*?
7. Do peanuts grow above or below ground?
8. In which US state can you find the popular holiday destination of Orlando?
9. Are the three main ingredients of a classic Margherita pizza cheese and tomato with ham, basil or pepperoni?
10. Which cartoon character lives in a pineapple at the bottom of the sea?
11. Who introduces the Channel 4 programme *Deal Or No Deal*?
12. Name the ex-England footballer and the Welsh singer who featured in a series of TV advertisments for crisps.
13. What kind of creature is the puppet, Basil Brush?
14. Did the Great Fire of London start in: a) Soup Lane, b) Fish Lane, c) Pie Lane or d) Pudding Lane?
15. According to the name of the cartoon series, what is Mona?
16. Did King Henry VIII have five, six or seven wives?

ANSWERS

1 Paris, 2 Only lean, 3 Ron Weasley and Hermione Granger, 4 Dennis is the only one who isn't one of the Bash Street Kids, 5 EastEnders, 6 He is a pig who can herd sheep like a dog, 7 Below, 8 Florida, 9 Cheese with tomato and basil, 10 SpongeBob SquarePants, 11 Noel Edmonds, 12 Gary Lineker and Charlotte Church, 13 A fox, 14 d) Pudding Lane, 15 A vampire, 16 Six.

GENERAL KNOWLEDGE

How much do YOU know?

1. What colour is the timber known as mahogany — yellow, pale green, or reddish-brown?
2. Who would be interested in a Cape Triangular?
3. First Class Post cost how much in 1980 — 9p, 10p or 12p?
4. If you went to a garage and asked for a 165 x 13, what would you be given?
5. On a map, what is the significance of a red triangle?
6. Where would you find the substance known as mother-of-pearl?
7. On what might you find gimbals?
8. Which tribesmen are found in Africa — Bedouins, Berbers or Bushmen?
9. How many people form a jury in a Scottish criminal trial?
10. Near which major city can you find the ruins of Pompeii?
11. How many pieces does each player have in a game of backgammon?
12. Pick the odd one out — Spike Milligan, Harry Secombe, Tony Hancock, Michael Bentine.
13. On a camera, which aperture size lets in more light — f16 or f4?
14. Is a casement window a sliding window or hinged at the side?
15. The Matiz is a model of car from which manufacturer — Daewoo, Vauxhall, Peugeot or Fiat?
16. The cut of meat known as sirloin is taken from which part of the cow?

ANSWERS

1 Dark reddish-brown, 2 Stamp collectors — it's a postage stamp, 3 12p, 4 A new tyre for your car, 5 It denotes a Youth Hostel, 6 Lining the inside of an oyster shell, 7 On board ship — it's a system of rings and pivots for keeping instruments horizontal at sea, 8 All of them. Bedouins and Berbers are found in North Africa, Bushmen in South Africa, 9 Fifteen, 10 Naples, 11 Fifteen, 12 Tony Hancock — the others were members of the Goon Show, 13 f4, 14 Hinged at the side, 15 Daewoo, 16 Behind the neck.

GENERAL KNOWLEDGE

How much do YOU know?

1. The royal yacht *Britannia* is berthed at Leith, but where was she launched?
2. Which of the following songs was a hit for Robbie Williams: a) *Angels*, b) *It's So Easy*, c) *You're My Best Friend*.
3. What word can come before car, wrap and bath?
4. What's the difference between a tigon and a liger?
5. Did Ralph Lipschitz find fame as a folk singer, actor, designer or film producer after changing his name?
6. Your timpanic membrane is more commonly called what?
7. Which patron saint's day is celebrated first in a calendar year? St Andrew, St George, St Patrick or St David?
8. Mrs Doyle was the housekeeper in which popular TV sitcom?
9. What colour gives its name to the longest river in South Africa?
10. Which of the following words can be typed by using only letters on the middle row of a qwerty keyboard — fish, dash, call or kiss?
11. On the Internet, what is *Wikipedia*?
12. If the temperature reads 68 degrees F, what is it in Celsius?
13. Bank of England pound notes ceased to be legal tender in 1988. But in which month?
14. What's the proper name for your voice box?
15. BMW cars are well-known, but what does BMW stand for?
16. Who was the last of the Yorkist Kings?

ANSWERS

1 John Brown's Shipyard, Clydebank, in 1953, 2 a) Angels, 3 Bubble, 4 A tigon is the offspring of a tiger and a lioness, a liger is the cub of a lion and a tigress, 5 As fashion designer Ralph Lauren, 6 Your eardrum, 7 St David on March 1, 8 Father Ted, 9 Orange, 10 Dash, 11 A free-content encyclopedia, 12 20 degrees, 13 March, 14 Your larynx, 15 Bayerische Motoren Werke or Bavarian Motor Works, 16 Richard III.

GENERAL KNOWLEDGE

Take the test.

1. Which Australian raised Hollywood actor has the middle names Columcille Gerard?
2. Did Marilyn Monroe, Winston Churchill, Charles Darwin and George VI suffer from deafness, stammering or clicking joints?
3. Name the first country in the world to introduce a law which made euthanasia legal.
4. Where was the Statue of Liberty built?
5. Which university in the UK was first to offer a Bachelor of Science degree in Science Fiction — Glasgow, Glamorgan or Greenwich?
6. What is the traditional salute to announce a royal birth in the UK?
7. Does a hedgehog have up to 1000, 4000 or 7000 spikes?
8. How many barrels of gunpowder were found when Guy Fawkes tried to blow up the Houses of Parliament — 16, 36, 56 or 76?
9. Which weird US TV comedy family shared its name with an Irish province?
10. What are the basic ingredients of a tortilla or Spanish omlette?
11. Arthur Philip Louis are the other names of which royal?
12. Which famous Hitchcock movie was chiefly set in a place called Bodega Bay?
13. Which crime fiction board game was devised by A Pratt in 1948?
14. Which fictional train travels through Grumbly Town?
15. We've all heard of German football team Bayern Munich, but what is Bayern in English?
16. What word links a summer sport with a noisy insect?

ANSWERS

1 Mel Gibson, 2 Stammering, 3 The Netherlands, in 2000, 4 In France, as a gift to the people of the USA, 5 Glamorgan, 6 A 41-gun salute, 7 Up to 7000, 8 36, 9 The Munsters, Munster is an Irish province, 10 Eggs with potatoes and onions, 11 Prince William, 12 The Birds, 13 Cluedo, 14 Ivor the Engine, 15 Bavaria, 16 Cricket.

SPORT
Actively awesome!

1. Meadowlark Lemon was a famous name in which sport? Basketball, tennis or American football?
2. In which sport would you find the terms 'running', 'tacking' and 'broaching'?
3. Who won the World Snooker Championship in 2006?
4. What nationality is golfer Niclas Fasth?
5. How many players form a scrum in Rugby Union?
6. What was the venue for the 2005 Open Golf Championship?
7. Who handles the ball first in an American football 'down'?
8. Which boxer claimed to 'float like a butterfly and sting like a bee'?
9. In which city do soccer side Port Vale play?
10. Who was the highest wicket-taker in the 2007 cricket World Cup?
11. In a relay race, what is the term given for the last man to run?
12. What is the name of Real Madrid's stadium?
13. With which sport would you associate Miguel Indurain?
14. *I'm Forever Blowing Bubbles* is a song associated with which English football club?
15. 'Wipeout' is a term used in baseball, surfing or wrestling?
16. Which England cricket county is based at Edgbaston?

ANSWERS

1 Basketball, 2 Sailing, 3 Graham Dott, 4 Swedish, 5 Sixteen, 6 St Andrews, 7 The Centre, 8 Muhammad Ali, 9 Stoke-on-Trent, 10 Glenn McGrath, 11 Anchorman, 12 Santiago Bernabeu, 13 Cycling, 14 West Ham United, 15 Surfing, 16 Warwickshire.

GENERAL KNOWLEDGE

Facts are fun!

1. Name the three four-lettered US states.
2. Unscramble NEVER STICK ON to reveal a Hollywood actor.
3. What is a clachan in the Highlands?
4. Name TV's three original *Charlie's Angels*.
5. Can you think of a sauce beginning with a country?
6. The following clues are for types of 'father': a) Mafia boss, b) most senior politician, c) country of your birth.
7. What are the International Vehicle Registration letters for Ireland?
8. Was Jimmy Carter, Ronald Reagan or George Bush the 40th president of the USA?
9. What is Sir Paul McCartney's full name?
10. Is a siamang a native of Siam, an ape, a tropical fruit or a boat?
11. What title connects a Lawrence Olivier film with a Kate Bush song?
12. Which animal only eat's the leaves of certain eucalyptus trees?
13. Is a harpy a species of raven, albatross, kingfisher or eagle?
14. What do the initials of the DVLA stand for?
15. Standing on the Salisbury Crags you overlook which Scottish city?
16. On which side of the road would you drive in Singapore?

ANSWERS

1 Iowa, Ohio and Utah, 2 Kevin Costner, 3 A small village or hamlet, 4 Sabrina (Kate Jackson), Jill (Farrah Fawcett-Majors) and Kelly (Jaclyn Smith), 5 Hollandaise, 6 a) Godfather, b) Father of the House, c) Fatherland, 7 IRL, 8 Ronald Reagan, 9 James Paul McCartney, 10 An ape, 11 Wuthering Heights, 12 The koala, 13 Eagle, 14 Driver and Vehicle Licensing Agency, 15 Edinburgh, 16 On the left.

GENERAL KNOWLEDGE

Quite quizzical!

1. *Trust In Me* is a song from which Disney feature-length cartoon — *Pinocchio, Snow White, The Jungle Book* or *The Little Mermaid*?
2. A bel is a measurement of what?
3. Born Maria Eva Duarte, this woman became known all over the world. Who was she?
4. We've all heard of a blacksmith, but what's a whitesmith?
5. According to the proverb, attack is the best form of what?
6. On the Beatles' famous *Abbey Road* album cover what iconic make of car is parked just beyond the zebra crossing?
7. Solve the following clues to timepieces: a) lady's figure, b) athlete timer, c) tall senior citizen, d) garden feature.
8. Princetown, Harvard, Mortice, Cornell. Which is the odd one out?
9. FRCS after someone's name indicates what?
10. How did the expression 'when the chips are down' originate?
11. Ivan is the Russian equivalent of which British name?
12. In the Paul Simon song how many ways are there to leave your lover?
13. Rearrange I BLESS SHY YEAR to recall a top international singer.
14. Where is your stapes — in your ear, nose, throat or brain?
15. Charles Edward Anderson is the real name of which 1950s pop legend?
16. It's called Summer Time in the UK, but how is it known in the US?

ANSWERS

1 The Jungle Book, 2 Sound, 3 Eva Peron — or Evita, 4 A craftsman who works with tin, or a polisher of metals, 5 Defence, 6 Volkswagen Beetle, 7 a) Hourglass, b) stopwatch, c) grandfather clock, d) sundial, 8 Mortice is a type of lock, while the others are American universities, 9 He or she is a Fellow of The Royal College of Surgeons, 10 From gambling, when the chips are taken down or away after you lose, 11 John, 12 50, 13 Shirley Bassey 14 Ear. It's a small stirrup-shaped bone, 15 Chuck Berry, 16 Daylight Saving Time.

The SUNDAY POST FAMILY QUIZ BOOK

GENERAL KNOWLEDGE

How much do YOU know?

1. What's unusual about a Basenji dog?
2. In the theatre, what is an oyster part?
3. What do crossed swords on a map indicate?
4. Solve the following clues to plants or flowers: a) does a lot of talking, b) sheep herder's wallet, c) always remember me.
5. Which is the only bird that can fly backwards — kingfisher, hummingbird, nuthatch or oystercatcher?
6. What colour are the gloves worn by snooker referees?
7. In what year was synchronised swimming added to the Olympics — 1984, 1988 or 1992?
8. A white crescent and star on a red background represents the flag of which nation — Cyprus, Turkey or Morocco?
9. Why is there cartilage around our bones?
10. Annie Mae Bullock found fame as a singer after she changed her name — to what?
11. How did the charity Oxfam get its name?
12. Imelda Marcos was known for her vast collection of what?
13. If your birthday is June 26, what Zodiac sign are you?
14. What is Little Nellie in the James Bond film *You Only Live Twice*?
15. In which decade were postcodes introduced in the UK?
16. *The Burrell Collection* in Glasgow's Pollok Country Park was gifted to the city by Sir William Burrell. In what line of business was he?

ANSWERS

1 It can't bark, 2 When an actor only speaks or appears once. Likened to an oyster you can only open once, 3 The site of a battle, 4 a) Mother-in-Law's tongue, b) shepherd's purse, c) forget-me-not, 5 The hummingbird, 6 White, 7 1984, 8 Turkey, 9 To stop bones rubbing together at joints and to absorb shock, 10 Tina Turner, 11 It began life as the Oxford Committee for Famine Relief, 12 Shoes, 13 Cancer, 14 A miniature helicopter equipped with various gadgets, 15 The 1950s, 16 He was born into a ship-owning family, but he retired early to devote his life to his collection.

BRAINBOX

For smarties only!

1. Does a petrologist study rocks, stars or fuel consumption?
2. Which part of your body may be described as retrousse?
3. Why was Pioneer 10's launch a landmark in space exploration in 1983?
4. What kind of acid is normally used in a car battery?
5. Cryogenics is the scientific study of what?
6. How long is the gestation period of a mouse — 18 days, 32 days or 45 days?
7. What are cirrostratus, altocumulus and cumulonimbus?
8. The term for the fluid surrounding an unborn baby is what?
9. How many vertebrae are in an adult human spine — 29, 33 or 42?
10. Who performed the world's first successful heart transplant?
11. Is an alloy a comrade, a metal composed of more than one element or an undersea weed?
12. Which two words that sound the same but are spelled differently mean a kind of boat and a part of a skeleton?
13. If you have otalgia, what is wrong with you?
14. What is the study of earthquakes called?
15. Who won the Nobel Peace Prize in 1990?
16. A coleopterist studies beetles, hair or deserts?

ANSWERS

1 Rocks, 2, Your nose. It means turned up at the tip, 3 It was the first man-made object to leave the solar system, 4 Sulphuric acid, 5 Low temperatures, and their effects, 6 18 days, 7 Types of cloud 8 Amniotic fluid, 9 29, 10 Professor Christian Barnard, in 1968, 11 A metal composed of more than one element, 12 Scull and skull, 13 You have ear-ache, 14 Seismology, 15 Mikhail Gorbachev, 16 Beetles.

GENERAL KNOWLEDGE

Facts are fun!

1. In what year was the board game Monopoly introduced? 1935, 1940 or 1945?
2. *Blue Bayou* was a hit song for Roy Orbison. What is a bayou?
3. Pertussis is commonly known as mumps, whooping cough or cramp?
4. What features on the symbol of the Church of Scotland?
5. What word can be a chocolate cake or a helpful elf?
6. Which popular garden shrub takes its name from Greek words meaning rose tree?
7. In radio communication what three words come after Alpha, Bravo, Charlie, Delta?
8. Pick the odd one out — Cairn, Ashington, Bedlington, Border, Skye?
9. According to Mary Shelley's novel, what was Frankenstein's first name?
10. What is the UK's longest railway bridge?
11. Which of the following isn't native to Britain — rabbit, hedgehog or badger?
12. What would a thanatophobic be afraid of?
13. Are sea cucumbers animal, mineral or vegetable?
14. Bloody Point, Broken Woods and Sunken Meadow are all names for what kind of sporting venues?
15. We all know Sir Cliff Richard's real name is Harry Webb, but what's his middle name?
16. According to the nursery rhyme, how much shall Johnny's new master pay him?

ANSWERS

1 1935, 2 A swampy, breakaway mass of water, by a lake or river, 3 Whooping cough, 4 The burning bush, 5 A brownie, 6 Rhododendron, 7 Echo, Foxtrot, Golf, 8 Ashington. The others are types of terrier, 9 Victor, 10 The Tay Railway Bridge at just over two miles long, 11 The rabbit, introduced from France in the 12th Century, 12 Death, 13 Animal, 14 Golf courses in America, 15 Roger, 16 A penny a day.

THE SUNDAY POST
FAMILY
QUIZ BOOK

GENERAL KNOWLEDGE

Take the test.

1. What are 'Belties' in south-west Scotland?
2. Who had a koala puppet called Coojeebear?
3. Which tennis-playing sister is older — Venus or Serena Williams?
4. Which Scottish bank has issued notes featuring Robert Burns, Mary Slessor and Robert the Bruce?
5. What's meant by the words distaff and spear on a family tree?
6. How would an American probably refer to a curriculum vitae?
7. How many legs should support a grand piano?
8. Solve the following clues to flowers: a) card game and mythical beast, b) sugary vegetable, c) part of your eye.
9. What's the correct way to attract a waiter's attention?
10. Who presented the first edition of *Top Of The Pops* in 1964?
11. Is a dirndl something you would spin with a whip, eat, wear, or sing?
12. What is crowdie on a restaurant menu?
13. Is dizygotic a medical term for identical or non-identical twins?
14. What's the difference between a stutter and a stammer?
15. Name a proverb that contradicts 'look before you leap'.
16. What vegetable can be found in Eggs Florentine?

ANSWERS

1 Belted Galloway cattle, 2 Rolf Harris, 3 Venus, born in 1980. Serena, 1981, 4 The Clydesdale Bank, 5 Distaff refers to the female side of the family, spear is the male line of descent, 6 As a resume, 7 Three, 8 a) Snapdragon, b) sweet pea, c) iris, 9 Raise your finger level and try to catch his eye, 10 Jimmy Savile, 11 Wear, it's a style of skirt, 12 A soft cottage cheese, 13 Non-identical, 14 A stutter is repetition of words, a stammer hesitating over them, 15 Nothing ventured nothing gained or he who hesitates is lost, 16 Spinach.

GENERAL KNOWLEDGE

Facts are fun!

● 1-5 Could improve! ● 6-11 Getting better! ● 12-16 The best!

1. What was the first of Ian Fleming's James Bond novels — *Live And Let Die*, *Dr. No*, *Casino Royale*, or *From Russia With Love*?
2. Where can Scotland's 'Electric Brae' be found?
3. Founder Ingvar Kamprad's initials make up part of the name of which international home furnishings store?
4. Is oology the study of birds' eggs, odours, regional accents or ice floes?
5. How many symphonies did Mozart write? 39, 40 or 41?
6. Jedburgh Abbey stands on the bank of which river?
7. Which famous movie is introduced by the line 'A long time ago, in a galaxy far, far away'?
8. In The Bible, where was Jesus when he turned water into wine?
9. The malleus is a bone in which part of the body?
10. Landing at Luqa airport are you visiting Madeira, Majorca, Malta or the Maldives?
11. Kiss-behind-the-garden-gate is a country nickname for which garden flower?
12. What shape is each cell in a honeycomb?
13. The Lodge, Sandy, Bedfordshire, is the headquarters of which nature society?
14. Which king was killed at the Battle of Hastings?
15. Who wrote the opera *Dido and Aeneas*?
16. What do you call a young hare?

ANSWERS

1 *Casino Royale*, published in 1953, 2 Maybole, South Ayrshire. The brae appears to be rising when it's actually falling, 3 IKEA. The E and A stand for Elmtaryd Agunnaryd, the Swedish village where he was born, 4 Birds' eggs, 5 41, 6 The Tweed, 7 Star Wars, 8 Cana, Galilee, 9 The ear, 10 Malta, 11 The pansy, 12 Hexagonal, 13 The Royal Society for the Protection of Birds, 14 King Harold, 15 Henry Purcell, 16 A leveret.

KIDS' STUFF

Practically playtime!

● 1-5 Take a detention! ● 6-11 Take a break! ● 12-16 Take a bow!

1. In which French city is the Louvre museum?
2. What is the name of the first floor gallery in London's St Pauls Cathedral?
3. Who created Donald Duck?
4. What nationality is singer Natasha Bedingfield?
5. Who had a chart hit with *Brianstorm* in 2007?
6. Manx, Siamese and Bombay are all types of which animal?
7. What is the capital of Turkey?
8. Where are the Brecon Beacons?
9. How long is Hadrian's Wall? 71, 73 or 75 miles?
10. What is the official language of Argentina?
11. In which TV series would you have found the character Fozzie Bear?
12. Who played Indiana Jones' father in *The Last Crusade*?
13. On which river does Preston stand? The Ribble or the Rubble?
14. What is Paddington Bear's favourite food?
15. Who is Fred Flinstone's wife?
16. Who was the Maid of Orleans?

ANSWERS

1 Paris, 2 The Whispering Gallery, 3 Walt Disney, 4 English, 5 Arctic Monkeys, 6 Cats, 7 Ankara, 8 They are a series of hills in Wales, 9 73 miles, 10 Spanish, 11 The Muppet Show, 12 Sean Connery, 13 The Ribble, 14 Marmalade sandwiches, 15 Wilma, 16 Joan of Arc.

GENERAL KNOWLEDGE

Take the test.

1. The memory span of a goldfish is thought to be how long?
2. What is a cherry picker: a) an aphid, b) an American car or c) a hydraulic crane?
3. Solve the following 'Peter' clues: a) Opera by Benjamin Britten, b) Spiderman's alter ego, c) ex Dr Who.
4. If a photographer says a picture was taken 'contre jour', what does he mean?
5. When might you perform a tumble turn?
6. What is a chicken's wattle?
7. Can you float in quicksand?
8. Complete the proverb, 'More haste _____'.
9. Unscramble RUE BAGEL GUY to find a popular ball game.
10. Road signs indicating directions to tourist attractions have what colour background?
11. What type of pasta translates from the Italian meaning large tubes?
12. Identify these Scottish lochs: a) work for, b) reverential wonder, c) sounds okay.
13. Bramley, Baldwin and Braeburn are all types of what?
14. Is the right or left side of your brain believed to be associated with creative thoughts and emotions?
15. How did the foxtrot get its name?
16. How many furlongs are in a mile?

ANSWERS

1 *Three seconds*, 2 d) A hydraulic crane, 3 a) Peter Grimes, b) Peter Parker, c) Peter Davison, 4 *Taken into the light*, 5 In swimming, 6 The fleshy loose red skin below its throat, 7 Yes, if you stay calm and lie still on your back, 8 *Less speed*, 9 Rugby League, 10 *Brown*, 11 *Cannelloni*, 12 a) Loch Earn, b) Loch Awe, c) Loch Fyne, 13 *Apples*, 14 *The right*, 15 *Said to be from Harry Fox, whose 1913 Ziegfeld Follies act included a trotting step*, 16 *Eight*.

SPORT
Fit and healthy!

● 1-5 Bronzed off! ● 6-11 Silver lining! ● 12-16 Gold medal!

1. In which year did Virginia Wade win Wimbledon?
2. Which Scottish football club are called the Doonhamers?
3. Who invented the game of lacrosse?
4. How many players are there in a polo team? Four, five or six?
5. What nationality is Grand Prix racing driver Fernando Alonso?
6. In which city did Roger Bannister break the four-minute-mile in 1954?
7. In American Football, where do the Buccaneers hail from?
8. Which sport would you expect the Texas Tycoons to be playing?
9. On which golf course would you find Amen Corner?
10. In which sport could you win the America's Cup?
11. Was the Scottish Football Association formed in 1872, 1873 or 1874?
12. True or false — Andrew Flintoff captained the England team in the 2007 Cricket World Cup?
13. How many reds are there at the start of a game of snooker?
14. Name two 'extras' in a game of cricket.
15. Which two Italian football teams share the San Siro Stadium?
16. Which American swimming star picked up seven gold medals in the 1972 Olympics?

The SUNDAY POST
FAMILY
QUIZ BOOK

GENERAL KNOWLEDGE

It's a festive fizzer.

1. Why do we kiss under the mistletoe?
2. We have Sir Henry Cole, founder of London's Victoria & Albert Museum, to thank for which Christmas custom?
3. The infant Jesus was wrapped in swaddling clothes. What are they?
4. Boxing Day is also which Saint's day?
5. Paul McCartney and Wings had how many Christmas No.1 hits?
6. Name Tiny Tim's father in *A Christmas Carol*.
7. Alphabeticaly, which of Santa's reindeer comes first and which last?
8. Royal Mail expects to deliver around 1.1, 2.1, 3.1 or 4.1 billion cards, letters and parcels in the UK during the festive season?
9. You may come across a furcula in your Christmas dinner. What is it?
10. How is frankincense obtained?
11. How did pantomimes get their name?
12. What's the common name for 'Helleborus niger'?
13. Approximately how many real Christmas trees are bought in an average year in Britain — 4.5, 6.5, 7.5 or 8.5 million?
14. Rearrange WINS THE GREEK to reveal a popular Christmas carol.
15. In the song *The Christmas Alphabet*, what does A stand for?
16. Why is it inappropriate to fill your glass with Capo di Monte to toast the festive season?

ANSWERS

1 Ancient druids believed the plant had peace-making and forgiving properties, 2 The sending of Christmas cards, 3 Strips of cloth like thick bandages, 4 St Stephen's, 5 One. Mull Of Kintyre in 1977, 6 Bob Cratchit, 7 Blitzen and Vixen, 8 Around 2.1 billion, 9 The wishbone in your turkey, 10 By cutting into the bark of a deciduous tree and 'milking' the gum resin, 11 From the Greek pantomimus, 'imitator of all', 12 Christmas rose, 13 Around 7.5 million, 14 We Three Kings, 15 The angels who make up the Christmas list, 16 Because it isn't a drink — it's a type of Italian porcelain.

THE SUNDAY POST
FAMILY
QUIZ BOOK

ENTERTAINMENT
Test your celebrity rating.

1. What was the title of Fred Astaire's first film with Ginger Rogers?
2. Who wrote the novel *The Last Of The Mohicans*?
3. The composer Debussy died in which year — 1862, 1896 or 1918?
4. What was the alter ego of Don Diego de la Vega?
5. The musical *West Side Story* was based on which Shakespeare play?
6. In the story of *The Hunchback of Notre Dame*, what was the name of the gypsy girl?
7. Who was the male star of the following films — *Splash!*, *Turner and Hooch* and *Philadelphia*?
8. Becky Sharp is a character from which classic novel?
9. *Shakin' All Over!* by Johnny Kidd and the Pirates was a No.1 hit in the charts in which year?
10. What is the name of the actor who plays Charlie in TV's *Casualty*?
11. Which military sounding album was the eighth released by The Beatles?
12. In the film *Mrs Brown* who played Queen Victoria?
13. Which garden did Frances Hodgson Burnett make famous?
14. *Tainted Love*, *Torch* and *What* were all hits by which early 1980s band?
15. Dilithium crystals powered which fictional craft?
16. George Orwell's novel 1984 is set in which country?

ANSWERS

1 *Flying Down To Rio*, 2 *James Fenimore Cooper*, 3 *1918*, 4 *Zorro*, 5 *Romeo and Juliet*, 6 *Esmeralda*, 7 *Tom Hanks*, 8 *Vanity Fair*, 9 *1960*, 10 *Derek Thomson*, 11 *Sgt Pepper's Lonely Hearts Club Band*, 12 *Dame Judi Dench*, 13 *The Secret Garden. She was the author*, 14 *Soft Cell*, 15 *The Starship Enterprise*, 16 *Oceania*.

ENTERTAINMENT
Are you a star solver?

1. Solve the clues to find fish: a) a sharp pointed weapon,
   b) continually find fault, c) a high seat.
2. What was the name of Lulu's backing band in the 1960s?
3. Rearrange DO LAND ON NELLIE to find an Irish singer
4. Singer Bernadette Nolan starred in which former Liverpool-set TV
   soap opera?
5. Which ITV sitcom, which ran from 1997 to 2003, has a title which
   means too scared to go through with something?
6. Who was often called the 'First Lady of Jazz'?
7. The song *American Pie* refers to 'the day the music died'. What day
   was that?
8. 'Tell me more, tell me more,' — what's the song and what's the show?
9. Rearrange SHUT THEN WASH BOOK to reveal a popular late-night
   arts programme.
10. Pick the odd one out — Runrig, Lindisfarne, Deacon Blue, The
    Proclaimers.
11. 'One for sorrow, two for joy,' was how the theme tune of which
    popular children's TV programme began?
12. Name three chart hit tunes with animals in the titles.
13. With which song did Abba win the Eurovision Song Contest?
14. Which film company starts its productions with a man hitting a
    gong?
15. Which TV detective was famous for: a) his lollipop, b) his raincoat,
    c) his waxed moustache?
16. Name three successful films with the name Ryan in the title.

ANSWERS

1 a) pike, b) perch, c) carp, 2 The Luvvers, 3 Daniel O'Donnell, 4 Brookside, 5 Cold Feet, 6 Ella Fitzgerald, 7 February 3, 1959, when Buddy Holly was killed in a plane crash, 8 Summer Nights, from Grease, 9 The South Bank Show, 10 Lindisfarne are a group from Tyneside, the others are Scottish, 11 Magpie, 12 The Lion Sleeps Tonight, Tiger Feet, Dog Eat Dog, The Cat Crept In, Horse With No Name, What's New, Pussycat etc, 13 Waterloo, 14 J Arthur Rank, 15 a) Kojak, b) Colombo, c) Poirot, 16 Saving Private Ryan, Ryan's Daughter, Von Ryan's Express.

SUNDAY POST
FAMILY
QUIZ BOOK

GENERAL KNOWLEDGE

Quite quizzical!

1. Name three flightless birds.
2. What term refers to a person appointed to vote in place of another?
3. Which famous British public school begins with a boy's name?
4. What was the first name of F Scott Fitzgerald? Francis, Fred or Fielding?
5. Is a mudskipper a beachcombing machine, a submarine captain or a species of fish?
6. What do they call candy floss in the United States?
7. What kind of animal was Beatrix Potter's Mrs Tiggywinkle?
8. Why do we 'bite the bullet' when we do something courageous?
9. On which golf course would you find the Postage Stamp hole? Turnberry, Troon or St Andrews?
10. Which instruments constitute a string quartet?
11. The *Town of Titipu* is the alternative name for which Gilbert and Sullivan operetta?
12. Where would you find a Plimsoll Line?
13. Who wrote *The Waverley Novels*?
14. What nationality is singer Kiri te Kanawa?
15. In which Russian city could you see the Italian Bridge?
16. Which country was previously known as The Gold Coast?

ANSWERS

1 Emu, penguin, ostrich, cassowary, rhea or kiwi, 2 By proxy, 3 Gordonstoun, 4 Francis, 5 A species of fish, 6 Cotton candy, 7 A hedgehog, 8 From wounded soldiers biting on a bullet when being treated without anaesthetic, 9 Troon, 10 Two violins, a viola and a cello, 11 The Mikado, 12 On a ship. It gauges the weight of the cargo, 13 Sir Walter Scott, 14 She is from New Zealand, 15 St Petersburg, 16 Ghana.

GENERAL KNOWLEDGE

Take the test.

● 1-5 Must try harder! ● 6-11 Could do better! ● 12-16 Top of the class!

1. The musical *Kiss Me, Kate* is based on which Shakespearean play?
2. What colour are Harrods carrier bags?
3. Which member of the Royal Family opened the Tay Road Bridge?
4. What kind of food is galantine?
5. Who composed the opera *The Marriage of Figaro*?
6. To which island was Napoleon finally banished?
7. The site of the Battle of Waterloo is in which modern day country?
8. Where would you be most likely to find a brigantine?
9. Which 1980s musical trio took their name from a pair of bumbling detectives in the *Adventures Of Tintin* cartoon?
10. Benny the Ball was an acquaintance of which TV cartoon character?
11. What is the highest mountain in Japan?
12. Who wrote the novel *For Whom the Bell Tolls*?
13. True or false — Annapurna is the second highest mountain in the World?
14. Which is the fourth book in the Old Testament?
15. Who was known as The Desert Fox?
16. Which author's last complete works include *Pictures From Italy* and *Master Humphrey's Clock*?

━━━━━━━ **ANSWERS** ━━━━━━━

The SUNDAY POST
FAMILY
QUIZ BOOK

GENERAL KNOWLEDGE
Facts are fun!

1. What and where is the world's highest lake?
2. If you asked for la cuenta in a Spanish restaurant what would the waiter bring you?
3. How old was Western outlaw Billy The Kid when he was shot?
4. Which make of car is also a city in Uruguay — Mercedes, Volvo, Kia or Jaguar?
5. What follows these words from the famous hymn, 'Abide with me _____'?
6. If you were in the Gare St Lazaire, which city would you be in?
7. Name the hits by the following artists with 'prayer' in the title:
   a) Bon Jovi, b) Madonna, c) Aretha Franklin, d) Texas.
8. EH Shepherd is probably best known for illustrating which series of children's books?
9. The flag of Monaco is blue and white, green and white or red and white?
10. Which river flows through Washington?
11. Whereabouts in the human eye is the sclera?
12. Name the most famous presenter of the TV series *Top Gear*?
13. Which two US states share a border with Florida?
14. In January 1924 the city of Petrograd changed its name. What did it change to, and why?
15. What is the city of Hull's full name?
16. What are the Roman numerals for 900?

ANSWERS

1 Lake Titicaca, on the Peru-Bolivia border, 2 The bill, 3 He was 21, 4 Mercedes, 5 'Fast falls the eventide', 6 Paris, 7 a) Livin' On A Prayer, b) Like A Prayer, c) I Say A Little Prayer, d) Prayer For You, 8 Winnie The Pooh, 9 Red and white, 10 The Potomac, 11 It's the white outer coat of the eyeball, 12 Jeremy Clarkson, 13 Georgia and Alabama, 14 Petrograd became Leningrad following the death of Lenin. It changed again, to St Petersburg, in 1991, 15 Kingston-Upon-Hull 16 CM.

GENERAL KNOWLEDGE

Quite quizzical!

● 1-5 Quite quiet! ● 6-11 Quite qualified! ● 12-16 Quite quick!

1. If someone gave you a 'sockeye' would you wear it, eat it, or plant it in your garden?
2. Pick the odd one out — grey squirrel, mink, rabbit, fox.
3. How did duffel coats get their name?
4. Should a rounders team consist of seven, nine or eleven players?
5. Which Scottish football clubs have the following nicknames: a) the Warriors, b) the Gable Endies, c) the Blue Brazil?
6. William Henry Pratt found fame in horror films after changing his name to what?
7. Which words describe people who are: a) 40 years old, b) 70 years old, c) 90 years old?
8. Which exotic plant contains the name of a planet?
9. Name Scooby Doo's nephew.
10. Is the human stomach shaped like the letter P, O, J or D?
11. The following clues are for words containing 'phone': a) old music player, b) relating to speech sounds, c) not genuine.
12. What is a 'flitch' in a butcher's shop?
13. Who wrote *Wuthering Heights*?
14. What was the last battle of the English Civil War?
15. Hadrian's Wall was built in which century: a) First, b) Second or c) Third?
16. True or false — zeta is the last letter in the Greek alphabet?

ANSWERS

1 Eat it — it's a type of salmon, 2 The fox, which is native to Britain. The others were introduced, 3 They were originally made of a coarse material produced in the Belgian town of Duffel, 4 Nine players, 5 a) Stenhousemuir, b) Montrose, c) Cowdenbeath, 6 Boris Karloff, 7 a) Quadragenarian, b) septuagenarian, c) nonagenarian, 8 Venus Flytrap, 9 Scrappy Doo, 10 The letter 'J', 11 Gramophone, phonetic, phoney, 12 A side of unsliced bacon, 13 Emily Brontë, 14 Worcester, 15 Second Century, 16 False. It is the sixth letter.